THE HOLINESS OF
ORDINARY PEOPLE

MADELEINE DELBRÊL

The Holiness of Ordinary People

~

Edited by
Gilles François and Bernard Pitaud

Translated by
Mary Dudro Gordon
and Abigail Tardiff

IGNATIUS PRESS   SAN FRANCISCO

Original text:
Oeuvres complètes, volume 7:
La Sainteté des gens ordinaires
Copyright © 2009, 2014 by Nouvelle Cité

Cover photograph:
Vintage Paris street scene
© Jack Tait/Alamy Photo

Cover design by Roxanne Mei Lum

Contents

Preface 7

Timeline of Madeleine Delbrêl's Life 11

We, the Ordinary People of the Streets
   (1938) 19

Our Daily Bread (1941) 29

Pagan Countries and Charity (1943) 41

Missionaries without Boats (1943) 49

Why We Love Father de Foucauld (1946) 93

Talk on Father de Foucauld (1950) 114

Liturgy and Lay Life (1947) 123

He Who Follows Me Will Not Walk in
   Darkness (1948) 142

The People of Paris Go to Their Father's
   Funeral (1949) 158

Mission and Missions (1950) 161

Church and Mission (1950–1951) 165

Preface

What is the nature of this collection? Some of its contents are already well known in Europe: "We, the Ordinary People of the Streets" and also "Missionaries without Boats" capture the very essence of Madeleine Delbrêl's spirituality. Other texts, such as "Our Daily Bread" and "Why We Love Charles de Foucauld", are not widely known because they were only partially published: whole chapters were omitted, words were removed or changed, and quotations were left out. "Church and Mission", on the other hand, was expanded by the addition of a few paragraphs from another text. Finally, a third of this volume is previously unpublished.

The 1966 book *We, the Ordinary People of the Streets* shares its title with the famous article from 1938. In the months that followed Madeleine's death on October 13, 1964, our predecessors wanted to make her work widely known—a goal, as we know, they did accomplish—so they borrowed the title of her previous article for the book.

Five of the eleven texts that follow have already been published. They were scattered among different journals. *Études carmélitaines* published "We, the Ordinary People of the Streets" in 1938. Then, in 1941, "Our

Daily Bread" was published in the collection *Encounters*. After World War II, "Why We Love Father de Foucauld" appeared in issue 4 of *La Vie spirituelle* in 1946. In 1947, Cerf included "Liturgy and Lay Life" in their collection *L'Oraison*, part of the series Cahiers de la Vie Spirituelle. Lastly, a short article titled "The People of Paris Go to Their Father's Funeral" was published in the June 17, 1949, issue of the weekly *Temoignage chrétien*.

In order to assess Madeleine Delbrêl's literary output during this period of her life, it is necessary to add two texts already published in volume 3 of the *Oeuvres complètes*: "Joys from the Mountain" in *Études carmélitaines* published in 1947, and "The Dance of Obedience" in *La Vie spirituelle* in 1949.

Some might be surprised by the lack of punctuation marks in Madeleine's writing. She used them sparingly and in a whimsical way. We have added the appropriate minimum for easy reading. The words underlined by Madeleine Delbrêl are transcribed here in italics.

Madeleine Delbrêl travels through history in an astonishing way. If her writings bear the mark of their times, it is also true that, as Jacques Loew has testified, "This woman was prepared by God for thirty years to help us live post-Council."[1] They are pages written for today, and they make for good reading.

---

[1] *Nous autres gens des rues* (Paris: Seuil, 1966), 9; paperback edition (Paris: Seuil, 1995), 9.

Over the months and years, a whole team contributed to the different phases of publication. Izabela Jurasz provided data entry in accordance with the archives. A revolving group of proofreaders worked on the different phases of production. The Association of Friends of Madeleine Delbrêl faithfully continues to provide indispensable support for the project and those who work on it. We thank especially the publisher Nouvelle Cité and their director, Henri-Louis Roche, who is working shoulder-to-shoulder with us in this long-term undertaking, which is an act of service to the spiritual life that transcends the bounds of a generation and a single country. We also thank Ignatius Press and their editor in chief, Father Joseph Fessio, S.J., for making Madeleine's work available to the English-speaking world.

An important note: These publications may reach some who hold still unknown and unpublished archives of Madeleine Delbrêl's writings. We thank you in advance for trusting us enough to make us aware of them.

Gilles François, a priest of the diocese of Créteil, Cécile Moncontié, who works for the Madeleine Delbrêl archives, and Bernard Pitaud, a priest of Saint-Sulpice, are responsible for this volume, and together with Suzanne Perrin, Laurence Tassi, Muriel Fleury, and Henri-Louis Roche, they comprise the publishing committee.

Gilles François
Bernard Pitaud

Timeline of
Madeleine Delbrêl's Life

1904 (Oct. 24) Birth of Madeleine Delbrêl in Mussidan (Dordogne), daughter of Jules and Lucile (maiden name Junière). Jules has joined the Paris-Orléans railway company and will be posted successively to Lorient, Nantes, and Bordeaux. He will become stationmaster in Châteauroux (1911) and then in Montluçon (1913–1916).

1915 Madeleine's First Communion in Montluçon. Her fragile health has necessitated special lessons. All her life, her health will be poor, and she will often neglect it.

1916 Jules Delbrêl is named stationmaster for Paris-Denfert in September. The family settles at 3 Place Denfert-Rochereau, in the 14th arrondissement of Paris. Madeleine (twelve years old) has been studying piano and writing poetry since 1914.

1920–1921 Studies literature and philosophy at the Sorbonne. Studies drawing and painting in a studio on Rue de la Grande-Chaumière. Madeleine describes herself as "strictly atheist".

1922–1923 Meets Jean Maydieu, to whom she is strongly attracted but who will enter the Dominicans in 1925. She writes "God is dead . . . Long live death".

1924	"Violent conversion". Her father becomes blind and must stop working. The family settles at 78 Place Saint-Jacques, 14th arrondissement of Paris, near the Church of Saint-Dominique. Depression for a year, treated in a hospital in the Vallée de Chevreuse.
1926	Her poems receive the Sully-Prudhomme prize from the French Academy. "Complete exhaustion" (cf. letter from autumn 1926 to Louise Salonne). She meets Abbot Lorenzo, chaplain in the European Scout movement, who proposes she become a Scout leader.
1927	Edits her poems into a volume, *La Route*. Gives up the idea of becoming a Carmelite for family reasons and decides to work for God in the world.
1928–1929	Sent to rest in a nursing home in Chevreuse. Health problems for her and her family until the beginning of 1930.
1931	Enters the École d'infirmières des Peupliers, a nursing school.
1932	Creation of the board of the "Charity of Jesus"
	Simple diploma from the École des Peupliers.
	Enters the École Pratique du Service Social (social service school) on the Boulevard Montparnasse in Paris.

1933 (Sept.)	First trip to Rome, just after deciding to establish the first team in Ivry. Madeleine suffers greatly from stomach problems.
(Oct.)	Commitment to the Charity of Jesus with Suzanne Lacloche and Hélène Manuel at Saint Jean-Baptiste Church in Ivry: to live the Gospel and to serve the parishes. Moves onto the parish grounds, 207 route de Choisy.
1934	Abbot Lorenzo is named vicar of Ivry.
	First exam at the École Pratique du Service Social, passes with honors.
	Summer camp. Terrible health.
1935	(April) Moves to 11 rue Raspail in Ivry.
1936	After years of spousal discord, the Delbrêls separate. Jules moves to Mussidan, and Madame Delbrêl moves to Paris. Madeleine continues to take care of them.
(Nov.)	Second exam at the École Pratique de Service Social, passes with honors.
1937	Certificate for Professional Social Service Worker. Her memoir about the end of her studies, *Ampleur et dépendance du service social*, is published by Bloud et Gay.
1938–1939	Gives talks to a variety of audiences.
1939	(Sept.) Madeleine is hired by the GASSS and appointed social worker at Ivry City Hall.

1940

The Communist municipality is deposed. The small Communist staff remains in place. Madeleine is named technical delegate in charge of coordinating social services in Ivry.

1941

Enters into social service for the Parisian region (until October 1, 1945). Hires staff for the National Relief organization.

(summer)

Madeleine accompanies her mother to Lisieux, where she meets Father Augros, superior of the future seminary for the Mission de France, which has just been founded.

1942

Participates in conferences in Lisieux at the seminary for the Mission de France, but refuses to establish a team there.

1943

An important year for the Charity of Jesus' guidelines. The team includes Christine de Boismarmin, Louise Brunot, Germaine Gérôme, Marie-Aimée Jouvenet, Raymonde Kanel, Suzanne Lacloche, Hélène Manuel, Paulette Penchenier, Suzanne Perrin, Andrée Saussac, Marthe Sauvageot, and Andrée Voillot.

Establishment of Marthe Sauvageot and Suzanne Lacloche in Cerisiers (Yonne), and of Christine de Boismarmin, Paulette Penchenier, and Suzanne Perrin in Vernon (Eure) until the Liberation in 1945.

1944

Ivry City Hall is taken back by the Communists. Madeleine works with the "big guys of the Party".

1944–1945   Beginning of collaboration with Venise Gosnat, assistant to the mayor of Ivry. In October, she stops working as a social worker.

1945–1946   Numerous poetic meditations.

1947–1950   Intense activity in the teams: in 1949, Hélène Manuel, Monique Joubert, and Suzanne Perrin leave for Herserange, in the mining area of Longwy.

1950   Meets Jean Durand, semi-retired professor at the École Centrale, who will help Madeleine on every level and especially with her family difficulties.

1951 (Aug.)   President Vincent Auriol frees Miguel Grant, former FTP (French Resistance Movement) member, who had been unjustly imprisoned and who had been defended by Madeleine since 1949, and on whose behalf she had requested an audience with the president of the republic in July.

1952 (May)   Second pilgrimage to Rome, a day of prayer at Saint Peter's for the unity of the Church. Madeleine meets Father Guéguen.

(Dec.)   Letter from Monsignor Feltin, on the subject of the Charity of Jesus, asking to see Madeleine on her return from Rome.

1953   (Jan.) Writing of a petition for the Rosenbergs, carried by a lawyer to Rome. They will be executed on June 20.

(summer)	Third pilgrimage to Rome during the crisis of worker-priests. Several meetings with Monsignor Veuillot of the Roman Curia.
	Semi-private audience with Pius XII at Castel Gandolfo.
(autumn)	Notes and letters about the Mission de France and the experience of worker-priests whose arrests were ordered by Rome.
1954 (June)	First conference for parish priests in Paris about Marxism, under the authority of Cardinal Feltin, Monsignor Veuillot, and Monsignor Lallier, whom Madeleine had met in the Scouts.
(Oct.)	Fourth pilgrimage to Rome. Called back to be near her mother after two days.
1955	Much work reflecting on Marxism, including lectures and an essay. Audience with Cardinal Feltin, who encourages her to continue.
(June 3)	Death of her mother.
(summer)	Fifth pilgrimage to Rome. Monsignor Veuillot gives the "Dissertation on Marxism" to Father Paul Philippe, O.P.
(Sept. 18)	Death of her father. Madeleine in very poor health.
1956	Madeleine lays out her notes on Marxism in order to write a book, all while giving lectures in the provinces. Her health is still

poor. Her draft, approved by Cardinal Feltin, is brought to Rome by Father Guéguen.

(Oct.–Nov.)   Sixth pilgrimage to Rome. Monsignor Veuillot and Father Paul Philippe approve the publication.

1957   (Feb.) Seventh pilgrimage to Rome to discuss the fourth part of the book with Monsignor Veuillot.

Revision of the four parts and appendixes without rest until March. The book will be called *Ville marxiste, terre de mission* (Marxist city, mission territory). The first author's copies are sent in September.

1958   Death of Father Lorenzo.

Eighth pilgrimage to Rome. General Audience with Pius XII.

Development of the charter of the Charity of Jesus by Monsignor Veuillot and decision to relinquish the idea of a secular institute envisioned for the past two years.

(summer)   Ninth pilgrimage to Rome. Initial thoughts about Africa.

1959   Tenth pilgrimage to Rome. Monsignor Veuillot is named bishop of Angers.

1960 (March)   Madeleine refuses to join in welcoming Khrushchev to Ivry City Hall.

1960–1961   Lectures on Marxism given in diverse milieus.

1961   (Nov.) Departure of Suzanne Perrin and Guitemie Galmiche for Abidjan.

        Trip to Poland.

1962   Madeleine is asked by a former bishop of Tananarive to write a work on contemporary atheism in view of the Council.

        Father Loew agrees to relieve partially Monsignor Veuillot, who has been appointed coadjutor archbishop to Cardinal Feltin, in order to take care of the teams.

1963–1964   Writings and lectures about atheism.

1964   (Oct. 13) Sudden death of Madeleine.

1988   Monsignor Frétellière, bishop of Créteil, decides to open the cause for the beatification of Madeleine Delbrêl.

1996   The cause is recognized as valid by Rome. Madeleine is declared a "Servant of God".

2018   Madeleine is declared "Venerable" by Pope Francis.

We, the Ordinary People
of the Streets (1938)

At the end of 1937, the Charity of Jesus, which is the name of the group of women Madeleine Delbrêl had been involved with in Ivry-sur-Seine since 1933, saw its membership double. There were three members in 1933 and 1934. In 1935, six participated in the September retreat, but only three remained involved. There was one admission in 1936 and four in 1937. It was thus on behalf of eight women that Madeleine Delbrêl wrote, in January 1938, *"Nous autres gens des rues"* (We, the ordinary people of the streets) for the journal *Études carmélitaines*. And she submitted it discreetly, signing the article "M.D."

This signature was accompanied by an important note that deserves to be read carefully: "These remarks come to us from a group of lay people from the suburbs: souls determined to live the Gospel without limit. These souls cannot stand unrealism: their apostolate is one of life. Their method is not to work for Christ but to relive Christ in the midst of a de-Christianized world. To this end, this group aims to be acted upon, not to act."

These women defined themselves as a "group of lay people from the suburbs". The type of commitment is new, for these are lay people. The mission field is also new—the suburbs of Paris—because awareness of the de-Christianization of the world had been increasing for some years. The tone immediately taps into the deep mystical vein that nourishes the missionaries: to be acted upon, because it is God who acts. Madeleine Delbrêl wrote in 1943, in *"Pays païens et charité"* (Pagan countries and charity), one of the readings in this volume, about "actions that are a glove of very soft leather on the fingers of the Holy Spirit". It is the hand that acts, not the glove. The group took this direction in 1931. They wanted to be "less animated by a very active missionary spirit than desirous of living as de Foucauld did. No longer to 'work for Christ' but 'to be Christ, in order to do what Christ does.' "[1] Madeleine Delbrêl does not lead her group into action first and foremost. This may be surprising to the reader, but it offers him guidance.

This text emerges from a bubbling up of apostolic fervor that is exemplified by the title of the book *Le Christ dans le banlieue* (Christ in the suburbs)[2] published in 1927 by Father Lhande. The Church of Paris becomes aware of its suburbs. Energetic forces commit themselves to them. Although written on the eve of a war that would make communication difficult, *"Nous autres gens des rues"* would be widely circulated. The story of its dissemination has yet to be written, but

[1] For more on this idea, see *Madeleine Delbrêl: Genèse d'une spiritualité* (Paris: Nouvelle Cité, 2008), 57.

[2] *Le Christ dans la banlieue* (Paris: Plon, 1927). We do not know if Madeleine Delbrêl read it.

we know of at least two significant catalysts. First, the JOC (Jeunesse Ouvrière Chrétienne, the Young Christian Worker Movement) published some long excerpts from it in the eighth installment of a review edited by Abbot Henri Godin and put into circulation in 1943, *Le Levain dans la pâte* (The leavening in the dough), by Éditions ouvrières (The Workers' Press). Second, the young Mission de France, and its seminary founded in 1942 in Lisieux, was inspired by Madeleine Delbrêl. Its founder, Abbot Louis Augros, testified: "This text deeply inspired our formation effort during the first years in Lisieux. When the seminary was under way, Madeleine came several times to speak to the community, both before and after the Liberation.[3]

In all her work until 1964, Madeleine would extensively revisit the four themes that follow as subtitles below: silence, solitude, obedience, and love.

The following text is from a handwritten manuscript.

～

There are places where the Spirit breathes; but there is one Spirit who breathes in all places.

There are some people whom God takes and sets apart.

There are others whom he leaves in the masses and whom he does not "withdraw from the world". These

---

[3] Afterword by Louis Augros. *Nous autres gens des rues* (Paris: Seuil, 1966), 322; paperback edition (Paris: Seuil, 1995), 296.

are people who do ordinary jobs, who have an ordinary household or an ordinary single life. People who have ordinary illnesses, ordinary deaths. People who have an ordinary house, ordinary clothes, these are the people of ordinary life. The people we meet on any street.

They love their door that opens onto the street, just as their brothers, who are hidden from the world, love the door that has definitively closed on them.

We, the ordinary people of the streets, believe with all our might that this street, that this world where God has placed us, is, for us, the site of our holiness.

We believe that we lack nothing necessary, because if any necessity were missing, God would have already given it to us.

Silence

We are not lacking silence. We already have it.

If we lack silence, it is because we have not learned how to keep it.

All the noises that surround us make much less din than we do.

The real noise is the echo that things have in us.

It is not speaking that necessarily breaks the silence. Silence is the place of the word of God, and if we confine ourselves to repeating this word, then we can speak without ceasing to be silent.

Monasteries arise as the places of praise and the places of the silence necessary for praise.

In the street, pressed in the crowd, we establish our souls as many hollows of silence where the word of God can rest and resound.

In those crowds where hatred, greed, drunkenness reveal the presence of sin, we find this silence, the silence of the desert, and our heart falls into meditation with great ease, so that God can ring out his name: *Vox clamans in deserto*, "the voice of one crying in the wilderness" [Mt 3:3, Lk 3:4, and Jn 1:23, citing Is 40:3].

Solitude

To us, the people of the streets, it seems that solitude is not the absence of the world but the presence of God.

To encounter him everywhere is what makes our solitude.

To be truly alone[4] is, for us, to participate in the solitude of God. He is so great that he leaves no room for anyone else unless in him. The whole world is like a vast face-to-face[5] meeting with God from whom we cannot escape. An encounter with his living causality in these street corners bustling with movement.[6]

An encounter with his imprint on the earth.

[4] A few noticeable differences appear between the text from *Études carmélitaines* and the handwritten manuscript. We are noting the main ones based on the handwritten text.

[5] *Études carmélitaines* has ". . . a face to face with him. . . ."

[6] *Études carmélitaines*: ". . . movements".

An encounter with his providence in the laws of science.

An encounter with Christ in all these "little ones who belong to him", those who suffer in their bodies, those who are bored, those who worry, those who are in need.

An encounter with Christ rejected, in the sin of a thousand faces. How could we have the heart to mock them or to hate these many sinners with whom we rub shoulders?

The solitude of God in fraternal charity: Christ serving Christ. Christ in the one who serves, Christ in the one who is served.

How could discipleship be a waste of energy or a distraction for us?

Obedience

We, the ordinary people of the streets, know well that as long as our will is still alive, we cannot love for the good of Christ.

We know that only obedience can establish us in this death.

We will envy our religious brothers if we cannot also die a little more at every moment as they do.

The minor circumstances (of obedience) are our true "superiors". They do not leave us alone for an instant, and the "yeses" we must give them follow one right after the other.

When we surrender ourselves to them without resistance, we are wonderfully freed from ourselves. We float in Providence like a cork in water.

And let's not put on airs; God does not leave anything to chance; the pulsations of our lives are immense because he has willed them all.

From the moment we wake up, situations that call for our obedience seize us. They are the ringing of the telephone, the key that does not work, and the bus that does not come, that is full, or that does not wait for us. They are our neighbor on the bench who takes up all the room or the window that vibrates enough to split your head.

Situations of obedience are the day's gears, one thing leading to another, the kind of work we would not have chosen.

They are time and its variations, exquisite because they are absolutely pure of all human will. They are being cold or being hot. They are the migraine and the toothache. They are the people we meet, the conversations that our interlocutors choose. They are the rude gentleman who bumps into us on the sidewalk. They are the people who want to waste our time and detain us.

Obedience for us, the ordinary people of the streets, is to yield yet again to the quirky demands of our time as long as they are harmless. It is to wear the same clothes as everyone else, keep the customs of everyone else, speak the language of everyone else. It is, when we live together, to forget to have preferences and to leave things where others put them.

Thus life becomes a great film in slow motion. It does not give us vertigo. It does not leave us out of breath. It eats away little by little, fiber by fiber, at the old man's clothes, which are not salvageable and need to be totally replaced.

If we are accustomed to thus surrendering our will to the little things, we no longer find it difficult, when the occasion presents itself, to do the will of our department head, our husband, our parents.

And we certainly hope that even death will be easy; it won't be a big deal, but a series of small, ordinary sufferings, consented to one after the other.

Love

We, the ordinary people of the streets, are very sure that we can love God as much as he wants to be loved by us.

We believe love is not extravagant but something that consumes, and we believe that doing every small deed with God and like God is a better way to love him than performing great deeds.

Moreover, we are often quite wrong[7] about the greatness of our deeds. We only know two things: first, everything we do is little; second, everything that God does is very great.[8]

This makes us peaceful before action.

---

[7] *Études carmélitaines*: ". . . very badly informed. . . ."
[8] *Études carmélitaines*: ". . . is great".

We know that our whole job consists in not gesticulating under grace, in not choosing things to do, and that it is God who will act for us.[9]

Nothing is difficult for God, and whoever is afraid of difficulty will believe that he is capable of acting on his own.

Because we find in love a sufficient occupation, we have not taken the time to classify acts into prayer and actions.

We find that prayer is an action and that action is a prayer.

It seems to us that a truly loving action is full of light.

It seems to us that, before it, the soul is like a night that is very attentive to the light that is going to come. And when the light is there, the will of God clearly understood, the soul lives it ever so gently, calmly watching her God come alive and act in her.

It seems to us that action is also an imploring prayer.

It does not seem to us that action pins us down to our field of work, apostolate, or life.

Quite the contrary, it seems to us that action, perfectly accomplished where it is asked of us, grafts us onto the whole Church, diffuses us throughout her body, makes us available in her.

Our feet walk in the street, but our hearts beat throughout the whole world.

---

[9] *Études carmélitaines*: ". . . through us. . . ."

That is why our small acts, in which we do not know how to distinguish between action and prayer, so perfectly unite love of God and love of our brothers.

Delivering ourselves to his will delivers us simultaneously to the Church, who constantly makes herself life-saving and the mother of Grace.

Every docile act makes us fully receive God and fully give God in a great freedom of spirit.

Therefore, life is a great celebration.[10]

Every small action is an immense event in which Paradise is given to us, in which we can give Paradise.

Whatever we have to do: take up a broom or a pen; speak or keep quiet; do the mending or give a lecture; tend to a sick person or type on a machine.

All of this is but the exterior of the splendid reality of the encounter of the soul with God, every minute renewed, every minute enhanced in grace, ever more beautiful for her God.

There is someone at the door—quick, let us open it. It is God who comes to love us.

A request? Here it is: it is God who comes to love us.

It is time to sit down at the table: let's go; it is God who comes to love us.

Let's let him.

M. D.

---

[10] *Études carmélitaines*: ". . . a celebration".

Our Daily Bread (1941)

The following is an article by Madeleine Delbrêl published in March 1941, in the first volume, *Contemplation*, of the collection *Rencontres* (Encounters).[1] We do not know exactly how or by whom she was approached. However, Jean Maydieu, a Dominican, with whom Madeleine had a romantic relationship in 1923 before her conversion and never saw afterward, was the initiator of this new collection that replaces *La Vie intellectuelle* (The intellectual life). He was also involved in the underground press. Madeleine had a certain notoriety in social worker circles. Did he think of her to contribute an article?

Madeleine Delbrêl was responsible at the time for coordinating social services at the City Hall of Ivry and for the canton. She had just published, two months earlier, *La Femme et la maison* (The woman and the home), which was a passionate exploration of the true forces of society, focusing especially on women. *"Notre pain quotidien"* (Our daily bread) resumes this search with

[1] See the introduction by Claude Langlois to *Œuvres completes*, vol. 5, *Profession assistante sociale* (Paris: Nouvelle Cité, 2007), 45–50, as well as the study by Étienne Fouilloux, "La Collection 'Rencontres' (1941–1944) Jean-Augustin Maydieu", in *Jean-Augustin Maydieu. Actes des colloques*, ed. David Gaillardon (Paris: Cerf, 1998), 73–94.

a different approach. The former work is more practical, but spiritual enough all in all; this one is more spiritual but also very practical. Both display an ardent search for life, as France and the world were in bad shape. For Madeleine Delbrêl, every person could do something about it through "the minute and magnanimous accomplishment of our daily duty, of the duty of our state in life".

The text was published again in 1968 in *La Joie de croire* (*The Joy of Believing*). Unlike "We, the Ordinary People of the Streets", which was fully reproduced, "Our Daily Bread" was trimmed down. The chapter "Our Work" was removed. However, this theme took on great importance during the whole era of worker-priests. Moreover, some words were changed, such as the "duty of one's state in life", which became simply "duty"; or the "Catholic lifeblood", which became "the Christian lifeblood". The "good God" became "God". In noting these transformations of the text, our goal, of course, is not to criticize the first editors, who, too close to her time, wanted to adapt her writings in order to make them better known. But, with the help of historical distance, we wish to restore the thoughts to their historical context. The reader himself will take that which he needs from this work with a better understanding of his choice.

In the absence of the handwritten text, we refer to the text from *Contemplation*.

∼

There are some Christians who are Heaven climbers. There are those who are "earthlings". They wait for Heaven to descend into them[2] and hollow them out so it fits.

The size of Heaven in us is the meticulous and magnanimous accomplishment of the duty of our state in life.

The duty of our state in life is the opposite of what we might call the spirit of movement, of seeking.

It is that which hands over the small parcel of humanity that we are to the visitation of God and establishes us in an ordinance of love.

To do the duty of one's state in life is to accept staying where one is so that the Kingdom of God comes to where we are and extends over this earth that we are.

But to begin to obey the duty of one's state in life is to accept an obedience as large as the material of which we are made, the family of which we are members, the job where we work, the people who belong to us, the continent that surrounds us, the world that encircles us, the time in which we live. Because the duty of one's state in life is not a petty obligation, the way we sometimes speak of; it is the debt of our state as carnal beings, as children or parents, as officials, as bosses, as workers, as shopkeepers; as French people, as Europeans, as "citizens of the world", as those alive in 1941.

---

[2] A few differences appear between the text from *Contemplation* and the typed manuscript. Here the typed manuscript reads: ". . . descend upon them."

It is the full payment of this debt by the penny-by-penny offering of each moment that will make us righteous.

A tour of duty of one's state in life envisioned in this way would be a great journey, indeed. We will content ourselves with a glance at the first few steps of it.

Our Body

Our condition is to have a body. In the morning, as soon as we wake, our body is the first thing we encounter. This first encounter is not always pleasant, and this association, sometimes cordial, sometimes tempestuous, will continue all throughout the day. How many of us, in moments of overload or temptation, have not felt the strong desire to curse our body and have almost asked to be freed from it; and yet our body is not an accident. God desired it, God designed it. We have the nerves, the blood, and the fundamental temperament that he wanted. God determined our body in advance in order to make his grace dwell in it. He did not overlook any weakness, anything compromising or deviated in us, but chose to make up the body of a saint. We have the right body for our destiny, the right body for our holiness.

Our body is the site, in the course of the day, where incidents often pick a fight with our soul: the trembling of nerves, heaviness of head, good or bad moods—so many circumstances that are nonetheless circumstances and the expression of God's will for us. None of this is a negative that should tie us up or embarrass us. On the contrary, all these are the conditions of the coming of God to us; it is a bit of his will revealing itself: this feeling of well-being, this migraine, these tired limbs—this is the material of our grace of the moment.

We must get used to having a body as a kind of stewardship. It is the life that God entrusts to us, and we should lose it in the sense of a possession, but recover it because it belongs to him. We must regard our body as a farmer regards his land: knowing the value of our body, and esteeming it, as they say. Knowing its riches and its needs, what strengthens it and what weakens it, trying to harmonize it with these great natural laws that God invented and that we evoke whenever we want to describe the union between redeemed souls and Christ.

Our body does not end at frontiers that are easily perceptible to us. In this era, when medical and psychological studies often brutally expose hereditary traits or atavisms, it is no wonder people are troubled. They might feel themselves struck down, shaken in their desires for spiritual rectitude by these internal surges, tastes, instincts, personalities, passions, imbalances.

However, all these human mixtures are, in and of themselves, the material of graces, material for our grace. It is through them, too, that God decided to make saints of us. Nothing about them is worrying because everything is planned. It is a joy to offer to

God, as an offering of goodwill, this parcel of carnal humanity, which has come, through twists and turns, from the depths of pure or guilty generations—and by such an offering to be the body's custodian and to have the power to sanctify it.

It is very expanding to know that our will, applied to the will of God, is enough to put this whole mass of humanity in order: our will should be both firm and tender, extended toward God and released of its own rigidity, like a sheath of well-tanned leather that becomes as hard[3] as the blade we encase with it.

This discovery of the will of God in our body means that we should consider the least part of it with respect. There is a certain reverence due to that which God has made. There is no need to fear that we will thereby materialize our lives. Instead, the reverence we give to the action of God in our flesh will lead us deeply to adore the work that he undertakes in souls. The justice that we practice toward our body will perhaps make us more just toward our soul.

Our Work

Work is love.

It is the simplest, the most constant, the most real act of fraternal charity.

Christ did not disdain to give the greater part of his life to work.

---

[3] Typed manuscript: ". . . becomes as pure as it".

We lose this sense of love when we make work servitude instead of making it service.

We cannot work without serving someone: the one who extracts coal from a mine serves the one who warms himself; the city hall employee who draws up paperwork from morning to night serves the one who, thanks to these papers, will receive money or help of some kind; the salesclerk serves the one who wants to buy something; the metal worker serves the one who needs a car.

And it is not a matter of how much or how little one is in contact with these human beings that constitutes service: nurses and secretaries equally serve their brothers because people need the work of one just as they need the work of the other.

Not long ago, I heard it said to a manufacturer: "A factory is made above all to bring joy." To work is almost always to bring joy somewhere.

Often, we would like to leave our work and go somewhere else, to serve others and to feel like we are serving them.

And so we go off to daydream about exploits God is not asking us to take on, letting minute after minute of the service God has actually chosen for us, and that has been assigned to us as our work, trickle by as if through a sieve.

For we have received this work from God, even if we chose it. These are the circumstances of our life, our skills and faculties that we possess as conduits to him. The rule of our work is like a familiar law of God.

Work, because it is love, is one of the great creative forces in the world.

It conserves life, protects it, nourishes it, develops it.

To work for one's children is to continue to bear them, to give them life.

To work in the sciences is, so to speak, to discover, to enlarge life and to glorify the one from whom all life comes.

To work to nourish ourselves is again to sustain life. We cannot love without working, but we also have to say that we cannot work without loving.

Thus we are able to answer the telephone all day, or provide meals, or type on a machine, or line up numbers, or buzz about a factory floor; we do not await some new activity, new horizons, or the occasion to make an act of sensational devotion, but we will surrender our arms, our hands, our intelligence to the spirit of Christ so that through us he will continue to love human beings, and this will be enough for us.

Our Daily Pain[4]

There is no accidental pain.

Our daily bread is given to us by the daily pain of some of our brothers.

Our daily bread and our daily grace.

---

[4] The words *peine* (meaning "pain") and *pain* (meaning "bread") are homophones in French. "Our daily bread" sounds the same as "Our daily pain".

In our daily grace, there is always a small part that comes from the daily pain of someone, somewhere.

There is no accidental pain; there is only our willingness that is accidental and that does not always want its pain and that skimps it, haggles over it, and botches it.

There is pain well done[5] just as there is work well done.

When we rise in the morning, we have our pain to do as we have our work to do.

And the particulars of that work are desired by the will of God, just as the particulars of that pain are also desired by the will of God.

We can do our work very well and not do our pain well.

We can easily control and check for flaws in our work. We will not know until after death what irreparable breaks in the edifice of grace were caused by the flaws in our pain.

When we do the will of God, when we get up in the morning, when we prepare a meal, when we go out, when we do an errand, when we take the train, we sink ourselves, so to speak, into union with the Lord in accepting and desiring his will.

When we feel the pain of our daily pain, when we get up in the morning with tired limbs, when it takes us ten times as much time and energy as it should to prepare the simplest of meals, when we have to cook

[5] More wordplay: "Done" and "made" are the same word in French: *fait*. "Pain well done" is a twist on "bread well made".

with smoke in our eyes from bad coal that won't burn properly and with our feet on icy pavement.

When we leave a warm room only to go into the street and slip on the ice; when we stumble all over the city, kicking up snow, to bring back—or not—the humblest of objects.

When we wait on a platform in the cold for a train that does not come, in addition to being integrated into the will of God, we become, through our pain, the givers of the grace of God.

You will tell me that all of these are the smallest of pains.

But we recognize an artist just as well by the way he plays a child's piece as by the way he plays the most difficult of concertos.[6]

Thus we would quickly recognize a saint in all these smallest of pains. He would bring to it an ease, a naturalness, and also a grace—in both senses of the word—a good grace that would make of this smallest of pains a work of great love.

He would have to love greatly to endow his pain with elegance, to carry his pain well, as we say, like a well-tailored suit that doesn't bind anywhere, that is made for you, in which you are comfortable.

We carry our pain like amateurs.

We play it like a piece that is too difficult, tensed up, looking at the sheet music, without style.

---

[6] Typed manuscript: ". . . the most difficult of concerts".

This devotion to the will of God in the smallest of pains will protect us from two faults that we would often be tempted[7] to commit against the "earthly" spirit we spoke about earlier.

The first of these faults is searching beyond our familiar horizons for the means of redemption for our world in need of it. The daily reconciliation of our overdrawn accounts of redemption is achieved by our daily allotment of pain, through which our accounts are balanced exactly.

The second fault is letting ourselves be deceived by the outer layer of our actions, like assessing the bark of the tree according to its surface area, its superficial appearance, without first making sure that the bark is completely supported by the roots of divine will, and without estimating its thickness—the thickness of our actions' pain.

Our truly active actions are these [the ones that embrace pain]: and these are also our universal acts. They connect us to the running Catholic sap and make us present everywhere man still has need of salvation.

Our little pains: they are, in the end, the marvelous means that we have of activating, of fertilizing, the great pain of the world . . . Nothing is sadder in this moment than to see the world suffering exceptional hardships blindly.

---

[7] Typed manuscript: ". . . be tempted to commit. . ." (in the masculine, whereas the text has this in the feminine).

And yet, these hardships are proportioned for the world just as our daily pain is proportioned for each of us. Also, it is a great joy to know that in "desiring" each of our little pains, we become the eyes of the sad and groping world.

Sometimes a single colorful vase brings out all the notes of the same color in the room that would have otherwise remained unnoticed. We might start to think that the good God looks at the world, and when he sees a shining example of an act of goodwill, he accepts everyone else's gloomy passivity as a worthy sacrifice.

A small pain voluntarily borne endows the astounding volume of great and universal suffering with a soul. It is through such pain that we help the world to do its penance validly.

We who are so fond of the news, so quick to interpret it optimistically or pessimistically—do we realize that the act of botching the way we handle our little bit of daily pain, of balking at getting up in the morning, at this tasteless food, at this numbing cold, is of more importance for the real history of the world than this disaster or that victory commented on by the voice coming over the airwaves?

Pagan Countries and Charity (1943)

It is 1943.[1] Madeleine Delbrêl has just published (in September 1942) *Veillée d'armes* (Armed vigil), a book addressed to social workers. The following notes mark a widening of the scope of her reflections, beyond the profession of social work and beyond the scope of "We, the Ordinary People of the Streets", which is the expression of a "group of lay people in the suburbs".

Madeleine Delbrêl is now in contact with the Mission de France. In the summer of 1941 in Lisieux, she had met Father Louis Augros, who would found the seminary in October 1942. She participates in the bubbling up of ideas and new perspectives that emerge from that period. September 1943 is also the year of the publication of *La France, pays de mission?* (France, a mission country?), the book by Abbots Godin and Daniel.

Over the course of the summer of 1943, a chapter of the Charity of Jesus is founded in Cerisiers, in Yonne, with a priest from the Mission de France. Another starts up in Eure in Vernon. These are de-Christianized, or never Christianized, lands. The Charity is never just an organization. Different instruments

[1] Christine de Boismarmin confirms this document is from 1943.

play the same music for everyone: "This music, which is alone in reality missionary, is the Charity."

Madeleine Delbrêl has been at Ivry for ten years. As a social worker, she coordinates social services for city hall. She knows everyone, or just about. For example, she is in contact with Monique Maunoury,[2] the young daughter of the war hero Marshal Michel-Joseph Maunoury, who came to live among the poorest in the Zone.

Paper was scarce—there was a shortage. Madeleine wrote on the back of unused flyers. Even though these notes are fragmented and written in block style, we have chosen to publish them.

~

What life in pagan countries teaches us about charity.

Some pagan countries.

In a single municipality, there are many countries.

Therefore [this is not] an objective exposé but some reflections from life.

I did not make these reflections alone but in a team with other Christians. That is why I will say not "I", but "we".

These Christians were led to the same reflections in the same terrains where they live.

The city I am speaking to you about: IVRY. 43,000 inhabitants.

[2] Additional reading: Marie-Clare Bergerat and Olivier Marin, *Monique Maunoury, un disciple de Charles de Foucauld in Ivry* (Paris: Karthala, 2006).

Geographically: hillsides and the Seine.
Previously: vacation homes, cows, vineyards, . . . etc.
Ivry Center.
Nineteenth century: The port and the train station, the factories, the arrival of new populations, the religious "equipment", the four churches.
1933: 300 factories, employers, communism,
Unemployment, tuberculosis, mental illness,
Families, childish dissipation,
Atheism, the "Godless", the parishes.
1936.[3]

The Missionary Offensives

Mercy	Rue Blanqui
Medical care	Plateau
Social service nurses	Maunoury
School	Rousseau
I. Po.	Madame Isselin

All this is excellent, but only to the degree that musical instruments without any work of music to play can be excellent.

While the instruments might differ, the music is the same for all.

This music—which alone is missionary, in reality—is Charity.

[3] Written in pencil in the right-hand margin: "*Missionary sectors*: Zone, factories, youth < Young Christian Workers, city hall, bourgeoisie, children".

And it is Charity such as Christ taught us in the Gospel.

It is long and slow to discern.

Yet it is clearly expressed.

But the darkness, our darkness, is such that we are slow to perceive this Charity and to receive it in its fullness.

It is of this Charity that I would now like to speak to you.

You probably already know what I am going to say to you about it.

But we—we have been very slow to discover it, and I think that among you are some like us, perhaps, who are slow to "see".

This charity is what most pagans remember about Christianity.

"It is true, we were told . . ." "It is true . . . that he said it a lot."

This charity is, to heroic degree, a commandment from the Lord, his commandment.

". . . as I have loved you."[4]

The cloak . . . the two miles . . . the strike on the cheek,[5] etc.

What have we made of it, if not a virtue among many other virtues?

This Charity is made using the whole cross.

[4] Jn 15:12.
[5] Mt 5:38–42.

While Christ made fraternal charity his commandment, he did not preach this charity until after having
preached penitence.

This charity is ultimately a gift from God, and it is
given to us to the extent that we have accepted that
the place we will receive it will be cut into us.

This charity should be universal.

All those who are sent to us.

This charity must be a charity of salvation.

Materialism and intellectualism.

This charity must be a complete charity.

People do not understand a specialized love that tells
them: I can give you this, but not that.

All the good that God wants to do to those with
whom we live.

Like a thread of a strap, the thread of the one thing
you do not want to give away.

A clear-sighted charity.

Because we will perhaps have trouble doing that
which we have seen we should do, but we won't do
anything if we have not seen it.

Here [there is] such a great necessity for penitence.

Time stolen from others spent in desiring for ourselves, in wanting for ourselves.

Love for the pure state.

A liqueur in many vessels.

Which finds its form in the needs of others.

No matter where.

Are you getting results?

When the Lord died, what results did he get?

We are not dead yet.

We think we cannot love without producing grace.

But this grace, where is it going, toward whom is it going? Toward what place? Toward what time?

God does not have to tell us.

Through the people close to us whom we love, at work, in our family, in the street, is the whole world that we have to love.

We do not truly love the whole world unless we love the people who are close to us in a practical way. But as for the results, it is up to God to decide the place and the time.

With regard to milieus especially impermeable to grace, to the Christian message, we would ardently wish for the multiplication of Carmels, of prayerful and penitent monasteries.

This wish does not cost us a lot.

Something more costly and immediately realizable is to hasten our own stripping [of attachments] and to let spring forth from this stripping a radical love for the world, the very love of Christ for this world and for everyone.

The love of the first Christians.

"See how they love one another . . ."[6] Not even "see how they love us"!

---

[6] Tertullian, *Apologetics* chap. 39, 7: "It is above all this practice of charity which, in the eyes of some, imprints us with a special mark. 'Look', they say, 'how they love one another'; because they detest each other."

The witness of the Christian community, so evident.

No matter where it is placed in the world: the prisoner's love, the deaconess' love, the priest's love, the magistrate's love, the shopkeeper's.

This love of God that made them give their life.

Love between them.

Love of redemption for this gigantic mass of dough to rise.

Love that was enough for everything, without feeling the need to leave for the desert, to invent rules, to do sensational works.

Of course the Holy Spirit wanted all that later, but as something added on. The essential for the salvation of the world was to love greatly in living and in dying.

Love of the martyrs—of witnesses.

Let us not deceive ourselves. A love like this is a costly, expensive love. A love that to be perfect demands putting our whole supernatural organism into imbalance.

You have to pray a lot to obtain this love.

God does not give the salvation of others to active people but to actions.

Not to active people for whom activity is full of bad leavening from our old nature.

But to actions, which are a glove of very soft leather on the fingers of the Holy Spirit.

The martyrs had a superhuman strength. It is asked of us to be inhuman toward ourselves and superhuman toward others. It requires God in us.

Joyful love.

Love of service, of prayer, of redemption.

A love that makes simple.

A love that makes poor.

Born of poverty, it leads us to her.

A love that makes us obedient.

[To be] missionaries to the unknown to whom circumstances will lead us, for whom circumstances will give us what we will have to give, etc.

A love that makes us pure.

The instrument of God for Salvation can be possessed only by him. All possession of it by anything else, being or thing, makes it unfit.

Revolutionary Charity among the world and even among Christians that leads us to embrace the evangelic message in all its rigor, in all its scandal.

Missionaries without Boats (1943)

Madeleine dates this text "The Feast of Saint John the Evangelist, 1943"—that is, December 27. For a long time it remained in manuscript form. The handwriting is steady, firm, and very legible. There are some strikethroughs, but only a few. The text is complete. It is even dedicated. Madeleine entrusted her *Missionaires sans bateaux* (Missionaries without boats) to the patron saint of missions. At that time, very close to the Carmelite monastery where Saint Thérèse lived, Lisieux was home to the seminary of the Mission de France.

Madeleine calls it a "small book". It is no more than fifty-two handwritten pages, written on the back of administrative documents, due to a paper shortage.

Two excerpts from this text were included in *Nous autres gens des rues* (We, the ordinary people of the streets) in 1966. It was then published in full in the year 2000.[1] Here it is now, taking its place in the deployment of Madeleine Delbrêl's thought. A question remains: Why did she not publish such a carefully completed text, which she herself referred to as a "small

---

[1] *Missionaires sans bateau* (Paris: Parole et Silence, 2000). Some excerpts from the text had been previously published in a little booklet with the same title, from the collection "Paroles de Vie" (Le Mesnil Saint-Loup: Le Live Ouvert, 1989).

book"? Was it because the war was coming too close to French soil at the end of 1943 to start publishing it? After she read *France, a Mission Country?* by Abbots Godin and Daniel, did she want to put into writing how she herself would answer the question? This is not the only time that Madeleine set about answering a question while remaining silent. Her oeuvre abounds with fully completed texts that were published after her death. She had, like other writers, an interior drive that urged her to write.

Are there other explanations for this non-publication? Her proximity to the Mission de France would not last. Abbot Louis Augros, first superior of the seminary in Lisieux, testified: "Before Father Godin's cry of alarm resounded throughout all of France, [Madeleine Delbrêl] revealed to us the depths of the pagan world that lives on our doorsteps, or rather in which we live. 'There are areas in France that are more thoroughly strangers to the Church and more paganized than anything one might encounter in China and black Africa', and she shared with us what experience had taught her concerning the fundamental requirements for Christian witness in pagan territory. And then she stopped coming. Why? No doubt she had the impression more and more that there was disagreement, or at the very least dissonance, between our position and hers." Actually, influences other than hers shaped the missionary impetus. At the end of 1943, she offered an inspiration that the Church was perhaps not able to receive. The outcry, sociologically documented, of Abbots Godin and Daniel, the first of whom also frequented the seminary of Lisieux—was it more accessible than the mystical reflections of Madeleine Delbrêl?

And yet, *La France, pays de Mission?* France, a mission country? was published in the collection *Rencontres*, the first number of which, *Contemplation*, included the article "*Notre pain quotidien*" (Our daily bread) by Madeleine Delbrêl. Had she thought that *Rencontres* would publish *Missionaires sans bateaux* (Missionaries without boats) after the book by Abbots Godin and Daniel? These questions remain, for now, unanswered. Madeleine was used to silence, and female voices were not the first to be heard at that time.

~

To Saint Thérèse of Lisieux,
patroness of all missionaries,
with or without boats,
may she do what she will with this little book
1943

I

Missionary Life

Missionaries without Boats

It has been said that there are missionaries in the Church. The same sermon every year urges us to pray, suffer, and pay for them.

We know that in boats from Bordeaux, Marseille, or Le Havre, they head off toward peoples to save.

We think that they should depart, and we should stay, that they are called and that we are not called; that they should take their boats and that we should read, by the fireside, the *Annales des missions étrangeres.*[2]

And the Church, in operation for two thousand years, across the world and throughout realms, is surprised to find her step so heavy, burdened with the weight of Christians who do not depart.

However, we do not have the right to choose between departing and staying.

We are inserted into the perpetual mission of the Church. We are the littlest finger of a huge body moving in space and in time.

Even when we are inert, others lead us and pull us along.

The Church is like the symbolic animal in Ezekiel. She runs in a tornado of fire. Whether we want to or not, we inhabit, within her, this tornado.

The wind that blows there carries the Church toward that which is not the Church.

If we became aware of it, it would lift us up, like wisps of straw, on its wings, irresistibly.

We who wave our handkerchiefs on the platforms to say goodbye to those who depart—we are unaware that we have embarked on the biggest boat in the world: the Church Boat. We are like blind, deaf, paralyzed helmsmen.

----

[2] Reference to a periodical review.

The sails billow in the tempests of graces, the boat docks in lands without crosses: sitting in a circle in the bottom of the hold, we discuss what is happening on the two square meters that are ours.

But the "Eternal Missionary" who is the Holy Spirit walks in our midst. In this hold packed with invalids, he reveals the essential movement of the Church. In our time he walks and breathes the hope of universal salvation into hearts.

Let us be taught by him.

Let us learn that the Lord comes into us like a path that leads him to others.

Let us learn that to receive the Lord truly is to pass him on.

Let us remember in the holy memory of the Church that the plenary encounter of Christ with a soul is simultaneously an encounter with the sinful universe, a candidate for an ineffable salvation.

Let us learn that there are not two loves: those who embrace God should have room for the world in their arms; those who receive the weight of God in their heart receive there the weight of the world.

Let us feel this hunger that grips the Church down to her very fibers, this hunger that is like anemia, the hunger of feeling how all the cells of her body live for her expansion and her total growth.

Let us surrender ourselves to this grace of awakening.

The sailor's son yearns for the sea. May there arise in us a nostalgia for places where people are not Christian and an obsession with the roads that lead there.

For if there are missionaries in the Church, she is a missionary Church, and we are the sons of this Church.

Lord, each of us is at one of your frontiers. In each of us, and nowhere else, you must grow.

Each of us is the sand that your stream must cross in order to go farther; the burnt wood that your fire must cross in order to reach another wood; the window through which your light enters the house.

Missionaries without boats, awakened from our torpor: Toward which lands without God are we going, by what roads, with what message?

Lord, we are going to try to understand: help us.

Social Countries

We thought that all countries were labeled on maps and that the black lines of railroads and ocean liners were adequate for going from one to another.

Living among men, we have learned the opposite.

While there are maps that show extension, those that show layers are also needed. People are classed one above the other like geological strata.

We walk together on the sidewalk: we come from two different worlds.

Side by side at a bus stop, this tattooed man and this proper little lady are as far apart as two continents.

In a neighborhood, walls and walls; a world of factories.

In the subway aisles, famous people, champions, stars: worlds of stars who, when we approach them, disintegrate into a powder of worlds.

In a train to the suburbs are half a dozen girls and boys. They pile together on three seats and make a beautiful racket: a country unto itself and better protected than China by its wall!

Civil state, rationing, charity organizations, hallways, counters, offices; Rue de Grenelle, Boulevard Saint-Germain, Rue de Tilsitt, ministers, prefectures, city halls, world of public officials, small and large countries contained by four walls in a suburban square, or behind a thousand windows in a chic quarter of Paris.

Somewhere on the Montagne Sainte-Geneviève: a room, three boys who think they are geniuses: world of poets, true or false, world of artists of all sorts.

Some men around a table where nothing is lacking: notebooks, numbers: world of business affairs.

In the train, pyramids of suitcases, people talking about tours, commissions, exchanges.

World of salesmen . . . and I assure you that it is a world.

And if this train takes us to Lille or Toulouse, to Quimper or Nancy, we will again find a multitude of countries, each as far from the others as Japan is from Canada.

Here, this will be the Mariners, and over there will be the Dockers, to the west will be the Charters,[3] to the east will be the Silk Merchants,[4] from the north

[3] The Chartrons Neighborhood on the banks of the Garonne in Bordeaux, once populated by wine merchants.

[4] Silk merchants spun silk in Lyon.

to the south will be the Gypsies, from the east to the west the homeless.

And in the midst of them all is the Church, the Church in motion "that stands at the door and knocks", and for whom so few of these countries have opened.

Solitude of the Church between these worlds.

Impermeability of these worlds by the Church.

Here the parish: little flock, happy in its faith, indecipherable to anything outside of itself.

Old church crouched like a bird, warming its faithful under its wings. The lights shine, in the early morning or the evening, on the coming and going on the street: nineteen out of twenty of those coming and going will not climb the steps.[5] The Parish floats in the crowd like a message in a bottle, sealed, containing a wonderful treasure and floating in the middle of the sea, with no interest from the waves in what it contains, until human eyes discover it.

Here, the priests in the crowd. Within them the Word of God, within them the continuation of Christ. In this train that they are taking, in this street that they are walking up, is the flock of lost sheep to whom they are sent, but none of these will come to ask them for this Word for which they live.

If we insulted them, it would almost be better, but we ignore them, we pass them by as we pass by the statues in our squares.

[5] The old church of Saint Peter and Saint Paul in Ivry is at the top of a tall flight of stairs, above a very busy intersection.

They speak in their pulpits: where the street does not go.

Even farther away are those who "profess" to love God.

Almost all have "left the world", and in the world we do not find them. It is necessary for the world, attracted by their light, like a poor butterfly to fly to them: but it is so rare.

The presence of the Church in these countries—it is we who can make it happen.

It is we who can advance her frontier.

If she is absent in so many places, if she is separated from what she seeks, it is we who betray her.

We who are the Church do not bring her where we go. We do not go where she wants to go.

To be a missionary is to have a common cause with the Church so that, in us, she reaches the extremities of the earth.

Countries

If in these layered maps God seems so absent to us, we think that on these extended maps, he takes his revenge.

On the map of the world, Muhammad, Buddha, Confucius share continents, but Europe is for Christ.

We think of ourselves as beneficiaries of a kind of salvation of the whole. Europe, for us, is a baptized land.

And much more so, France.

"First-born daughter of the Church", "Deeds of God through the Franks",[6] "France, land of Mary"— so many pious slogans that foster a national euphoria in our Christian hearts.

In this France, let us try to seek God.

In this France, which is truly a country and a beautiful country, is a beautiful creature of God. It has long been fashioned by a people taking on its identity.

And in this great country, so many countries that remain countries.

On its right arm, like a contradictory and valiant sword, Britain; on its left arm, like a crusader's sword, Lorraine; on its head, violent and realist: Flanders; on its entrails: the somber countries of the Center; at its two feet, like two light sandals: Provence and Gascogne, without conceit or wisdom. Such human countries.

Wide plains, like the heart of man; smooth valleys, like his arms; high mountains, trails, tragic like his thoughts; limestone plateaus and rocky hillsides rough like his desire; coasts as infinite as his need for God.

A totally human country.

And betrothed to Christ.

Some nations seem to have been destined for God or joined to the external splendor of the Church.

France, the "Frank", the "True", seems by its very name to be betrothed to the one who is the "Truth".

---

[6] "Gesta Dei per Francos" (The works of God through the Franks), was the title used by Guibert de Nogent (1053–1125?) for his history of the First Crusade.

Given to Christ by its vocation of light and teaching, of realism, incarnation, of active religion.

Is not its first Marian altar dedicated to the "Virgin who will give birth"?

Are not its saints mixed right into the dough of humanity: St. Louis, St. Joan,[7] the two Maries of the Incarnation,[8] St. Thérèse of the Child Jesus?

And Christ has left his imprint everywhere: market towns and villages called St. André, St. Pierre, St. Martin, St. Étienne; statues fixed to houses, crucifixes posted at crossroads.

He broke up the land into parishes where he had been a guest, in its dwellings, in bell towers, round or square, pointed or domed, of tile or slate, parishes of a few hearths or a few thousand men.[9]

But Christ, today, has withdrawn slowly, gradually, from this earth.

Entire provinces have thrown him out. Others are split between fidelity and apostasy.

Formally rural sectors undergo powerful metamorphoses: factories modify the human rhythm; new streams of population flood in. Faith is shaken. These

[7] Saint Joan of France, daughter of King Louis XI, foundress of the Order of the Annunciation of the Blessed Virgin Mary.

[8] Blessed Marie of the Incarnation, born Marie Guyart in Tours, brought the Ursuline Order to Canada; and Blessed Marie of the Incarnation, Mademoiselle Acarie, a Carmelite, featured in the history of Ivry.

[9] Madeleine Delbrêl erased the phrase that followed: "Such is the imprint."

are landslides where, without a dam, God will be drowned.

And in the cities, clusters of social milieus, in the neighborhoods where the large urban areas are becoming more populated, Christ[10] becomes the undesirable, the one who does not even have a record at city hall.

If things continue in this way, his kingdom will soon diminish, with only a few small islands of Christianity remaining here and there.

One day, this country that we proudly call predestined, will also say: "God is dead."[11]

And we will have let him die.

Perhaps because we will not have seen France as "mission territory", we will not have thought to be missionaries: whether in the countryside, in our villages, or in our neighborhoods.

Human communities were waiting for their apostles: we were those apostles, and we relied on others.

Roads

In order to reach these countries where Christ is absent, from which Christ has departed, we must set off.

There is no mission without departure, no mission without crossing the Christian frontier where we are.

[10] Madeleine Delbrêl erased: "Christ seems himself limited to his house, which the crowds desert, for many, he is the undesirable . . ."

[11] A quote from Nietzsche, whom Madeleine Delbrêl cited, before crossing out: "We will observe with Nietzsche, we will murmur Nietzsche's phrase . . ."

We have to leave the place where God is in order to go where God is not.

We have to leave as authentically as we would in order to go to Gabon or to the Indies.

The countries where we have to go have their languages, their customs, their idols. In order to break through there, we have to leave home behind: the language, the custom, the idols of our country.

It is always Christian departure that takes us outside of ourselves.

There is a place we must always leave. It is our Christian place: whether it is only us or an entire social network.

This departure is simultaneously a departure from our whole selves and an adoption of our whole selves by the milieu that is going to receive us or by the milieu of which we are a part without real fusion.

That is why there will be roads of all lengths and all types for us.

A road: this telephone call that will connect us to someone else's life. A road: the street to cross in order to visit people we have never seen; this stair to climb to go to the house of someone who, until now, we have only greeted on the landing. A road: the subway that we take together or the sidewalk along the factory exit.

The road: that of this girl who, because she loved a neighborhood of her city, has left her job, her family, and set up house in the middle of a strange milieu.

A road: the "detoxification" from her own milieu that she first endured before making any friends there.

A road: the little shack furnished by two girls in the midst of the children they were evangelizing, at an impasse, in order to live closer to them, more continually with them.[12]

A road: the job that leads us to the heart of the factory or to the most Godless office in city hall.

A road: the technique of nursing or healing that we learn.

A road of silence and a road of the word. A road of our clothes and a road of our homes.

Roads toward the future Kingdom of God.

II

Missionary Action

Missionary Mercy

Some missionaries depart for the ends of the earth to seek the souls hidden among the leprous.

The love of Christ, in "his body which is the Church", wants to reach all who suffer anywhere. Such a heavy inventory.

---

[12] In 1942, Monique Maunoury and Madeleine Deboissy moved into the Zone, in Ivry. Some children were soon permanently housed there. Cf. *Monique Maunoury, une disciple de Charles de Foucauld à Ivry* (Paris: Karthala, 2006), 8 and 43.

Where God withdraws himself, evil grows and pro-
liferates.

Countries without God are almost always countries
where poor bodies suffer, countries with all kinds of
sorrows.

"Bodies and souls": souls to save in bodies to heal.
People to console whose soul is starving.

Christ was present to all the sufferings on his road.
The Church owes her presence to all pain.

But at the bedside of all modern suffering, banners
without crosses provide the catalogue of organized
compassion: public assistance, departmental, communal, national offices.

In sordid, or simply administrative, hospitals, in asy-
lums where little old men prepare for their anonymous
death, in social services, in orphanages for foundlings,
near the infirm of every type: the place of the Church
is constantly shrinking. We barely receive her during
visiting hours.

She distances herself from suffering.

Prodigy of hell, mercy herself, this daughter of the
heart of God has become Godless.

Whole services of mercy have become social countries that await evangelization.

Make it so all those whose function is to care for, to
console, to heal, become, or become again, Christians.

Make it also so that Christians do not let themselves
be formed by a discounted ideal of mercy: those Christians who are doctors, nurses, social workers. Let us
speak clearly: may doctors, nurses, social workers not

content themselves with merely adequate work that puts them in the category of honest and competent people.

It is necessary to rediscover the face of Christ with all its intensity. There must be a revolutionary mercy in this mercy of the bureaucrat and the middle ground.

And this face of Christ must be brought to the ends of the world.

That is to say that when one is a Christian, one does not have to wait until one has gone to Lourdes on a national pilgrimage to see that there are sick, dying, and deformed people; or wait for the sensational stories in the newspapers to believe that there is actually a flood of suffering. Once we have learned these things, we must consider that we have a heart for sympathizing, hands for healing, legs for moving toward all who are hurt. We know Christians who show the face of Christ in one of the most sorrowful corners of Marseille, others in the miserable blocks of Paris, others elsewhere: but all this is so little.

The world writhes in almost *infinite* sufferings. It is the Church's responsibility to care for it.

The Church is like an anxious mother at the hospital door where strangers are caring for her children. She does not ask that we add a new sign that says "Church" to all the existing ones.

But she waits for us so that through us she can sit down at all these bedsides.

Let us not believe those who tell us: "The time of Christian mercy is past; beware of helping people too much, of rescuing them; mission work is not compassion."

Christ passed through, doing good in a world that was his own.

In us, he must continue to come, in this world that we want to be his.

Throughout the centuries, mercy was often the sign by which people recognized him: let us show him without alteration: our times will recognize him.

Missionary Justice

"He who does what is true comes to the light."[13]

If a society of Christians brings about a Christian civilization, a city inspired by Christianity prepares the way for Christian growth.

That is why those who work to infuse the spirit of Christ in the social body can be authentic missionaries.

The health of this social body is peace. This peace cannot be the result of chance; it is the "work of justice". But the human instruments that want to implement this justice must themselves be baptized, so to speak. Their baptism must be transmitted into the institutions, small or large, that are in charge of man's well-being—a municipality's charity office, a minister's committee, centuries-old administrations that are "unkillable", as well as institutions born yesterday but

[13] Jn 3:20–21.

destined for death tomorrow. The realistic peace toward which they work is the best of climates for yield-
ing a good harvest. A missionary is someone who creates this climate, as the one who sows, as the one who
reaps. The one who works for sound regulation of
apprenticeship indirectly, but effectively, prepares the
way for the action of JOC [Young Christian Workers]
sections.

And missionaries these Christians are indeed, whether heads of state or office managers, because of the
witness they bear in the midst of the work of countless
teams to restore or renovate our poor society, to give it
a heart that seems new and a head that thinks rightly.
Here are many people of goodwill. The thought of
Christ, plainly spoken, can open them to the light.

Lastly, they are the missionaries of nations. Nations
are made of judicial frameworks, of legal organs. To
Christianize them, fiber by fiber, is to return them to
the missionary task for which God has chosen them,
for which God keeps them in existence:

"Nations endure for the time it takes God to find
the elect to pull out of their multitude" (Bossuet).
Nations are made to help the sons of men discover on
"the carnal earth" what it means to become sons of
God. They are useful and humble auxiliaries of Grace.
The nations are missionaries to the crowds that com-
pose them, but they are also missionaries to each other.
There is an apostolate of nations: figures like [Ernest]
Psichari and Father de Foucauld have told us enough
about [this mission to] pagan peoples. But among the

old nations, instead of all the ghosts of Geneva[14] and
The Hague,[15] a Catholic action of peoples would be
desirable.

To be a missionary of justice is to prepare for it.

Missionary School

The place of the school in this mission without a boat
is just as important, just as essential as it is in the for-
eign missions, but on two conditions: that the teacher
be a real teacher and that he be a real missionary.

Too many Christian schools nowadays think their
first job is to raise [the students]—and then, if possible, to teach them. But this is a matter of loyalty: parents do not entrust their children [to the schools] to
be raised but to be taught. Not to respect the contract
is to lack honesty.

May they be real missionaries.

The school, in many de-Christianized and especially
resistant environments or countries, can be a magnificent mission post.

For this reason, these classrooms where real teachers teach should open right into the street or the road
or people's living rooms.

Independent school or public school . . . these are
two types of mission posts. One will preach . . . the

[14] Original headquarters of the United Nations, introduced in
1919 by the Treaty of Versailles.
[15] Headquarters of the Permanent Court of International Justice
since 1922, established by the League of Nations.

other will bear witness. I know of an independent school in one of the most atheist municipalities of France. It is run by sisters. These sisters do not wear habits. The whole neighborhood calls them "Mother", and yet they are such daredevils, so spontaneous, so simple, that except for their darker-than-normal clothing, we would take them for "average Christians". They really know how to run a classroom. But, at the door of the school, in a big kitchen, one of them peels, tends the fire, washes, cooks—all while receiving the whole neighborhood, which files through recounting its miseries, its successes, its joys.[16]

Outside school hours, children, older girls, mothers, and fathers come to visit. They receive them as they come, always kindly, often as the best of families. Nothing is trivial. They give them provisions and comfort; they advise and give shelter. The school is but a gateway into a boundless charity, conquering like fire.

If all the independent schools crouched beneath all our steeples were such relays of the missionary spirit, if all the Christian teachers were aware that they are "frontiers" between the Church and the pagan world, what could not be achieved, and what beautiful chapters in the story of the missions of France would not be written in the heart of God?

But one can be a missionary without being near a steeple.

[16] Reference to Sister Jeanne, from the Providence of Saint-Brieuc. The school was in the parish of Sainte-Croix of Ivry-Port.

Many lay schools, many high schools, have among their teachers souls who belong to God.

But, here again, we suffer from immobile frontiers. These are islands of the Christian life, not a campaign of grace.

And yet, there will be breaches that allow for breaking through to the Kingdom of God.

Breaches on the children's side. When an important person who is a Christian crosses someone's childhood, that can have unpredictable repercussions. Someone who, on the human level, is a true teacher for the child, by the sole fact that he is known to be Christian, can play the role of a trailblazer.

Again a breach, the formation of the spirit. What happens here is analogous, on a different level, to what we noticed in the legal domain. There is a culture that prepares the way of Christ, and there is a culture that impedes it. The teacher is free to transmit one or the other of these cultures.

Always breaches, resonances, often faint but also often real, in the child's family. The school is a powerful influence for the child. It has a prestige that overflows into the family, however little the family might lend itself to it.

Lastly, a breach in this brave but haughty caste that is composed of educational administrators.

It is the Kingdom of the spirit . . . And the Devil is spirit, the pessimists would say, with undisguised references to intellectual pride. But God—he too is spirit. And all beings who truly love the truth orient their hearts toward the discovery of God. Many of these people might have found their God if some of their fellow workers had smashed the ivory tower in which they work for their salvation.

Shoulder-to-Shoulder Missionaries

This is what we could call Catholic Action.

It was the great Pope "of the Missions" who was the Pope of Catholic Action.[17]

Why? Because Catholic Action is essentially a mission: the mission of being shoulder to shoulder.

We are very far from realizing in absolute terms, beyond our more or less flawed notions, what "the invention of Catholic Action" means.

The Crusades would be a very small feat next to a Catholic Action that was faithful to its mission.

The Crusades were a movement of religious character directed toward the Holy Land.

Catholic Action is a movement that is not only international, but inter-class—and in 1943, we know what that means—an omnipresent mission, radiating everywhere from within a social body, qualifying itself at every juncture, populating with Christian communities all that is human community.

It is a mission because it is an enormous conduit of grace, connected to the hierarchical Church, cement-

[17] Reference to Pope Pius XI.

ing, so to speak, the intimacy between the Christian and his Shepherds.

It is like a massive reaction of the mystical body to treacherous, or brutal, lesions that will not stop mutilating it.

It is like the body's hunger, the hunger adolescents experience when their legs and arms are longing to grow.

It is the pope's thought spoken in everyday words.

It is the truth and charity of Christ campaigning across the social universe.

But those who love Catholic Action the most think that it is still in its infancy.

In fact, this cry of "Everyone to the frontiers!" that is the profound cry of Catholic Action and that should make us realize how imperative our role as "frontiers" is only gets a response from a minority of Christians. We see Catholic Action as something above and beyond, when it should be the normal way of being an apostle in 1943.

On the one hand, specialized movements are still very unspecialized if we compare them to the deeply complex and nuanced reality of the world.

On the other hand, each of those engaged in Catholic Action is very far from understanding and realizing that the fate of Catholic Action is in his hands, that it will be he who makes it happen, that it will end up where he makes it end up, that it will start up where he makes it start up.

In the end, the spirit of Catholic Action asks only to

be embodied in young and courageous enterprises. All the shoulder-to-shoulder efforts in the neighborhood, all the shoulder-to-shoulder efforts at work, are anemic because they rely on the witness of a single Christian. Real Christian witness is communal. All those who try mixing with their peers to make a breakthrough would do so in a more authentically Christian way and with more grace if they joined forces with others.

Where two or three are gathered in my name, there am I in the midst of them.[18]

It is this presence that Catholic Action wants to bring to all parts of the world.

III

Missionary Callings

The Two Callings

Whether they are missionaries of mercy or justice, missionaries in schools or fraternal shoulder-to-shoulder missionaries, all missionaries are marked by a calling—but this calling is not always the same.

"Return to your home, and declare how much God has done for you."[19]

The Lord already said this to someone in his time, and he continues to repeat it to people in our time.

[18] Mt 18:20.
[19] Mk 5:19 and Lk 8:39.

In their hearts, he places such love for some of their brothers that it drives them to share their life with them, their whole life, in absolute communion.

They see society as the continuation of God's creation.

They believe that if society is to be sanctified, purified, it is necessary to "establish everything in Christ."

They truly love a cell in the social body, a cell that it is their vocation to make into a fragment of the mystical body.

They want to take everything in the world that is not sin and turn it into a place of grace.

They want to have a home like everyone else, built upon peaceful order. Within that home, they want a household full of tenderness. They want to be a peasant among peasants, giving to each thing its due, strong like the others, ambitious for a better tomorrow.

To be a worker among workers with the same workdays in the din of the workshops and with the same Sundays.

To stay close to those who gave them life and to surround themselves with those to whom they gave birth.

To live a faith that each of those they came to save can live; to live it thinking of them, so that they can live it in their turn.

To live it so beautifully, so joyfully, so supernaturally that everyone wants to live it.

To be a missionary in the social realm where one is born. To bury oneself like the grain of wheat in the humility of its providential soil; to die there to all that is human, and in full humanity, to be born to all that is the will of God.

To build the heavenly Jerusalem in the streets of Paris, of Lyon, or of Lille; on the hilly banks of the Yonne,[20] on the plateaus of the Eure; on the barges of the canals.

To be where God put them, from the beginning, like a little seed grain from which a whole field can emerge.

And above all, for nothing to separate them from this sinner, this pagan whom they came to seek by their immobile departure, that departure which commanded them simply to remain where they were.

To know that their boat can be their native home.

After those of the houses, those here of the road, the street, the paths.

They encountered Christ on these roads,
a poor Christ not knowing where to lay his head,
a homeless Christ,
a Christ movable in the will of his Father
like a feather in the wind.
A Christ without mooring,
Who said to them, "Come and follow me."[21]

---

[20] One team from the Charity went to establish themselves in Cerisiers in the Yonne and another in Vernon in the Eure.

[21] The callings of the first disciples: Mk 1:17 and Mk 2:14, but also Jn 1:39 and 43. But the whole quote is in the calling of the rich young man in Mt 19:21, Mk 10:21, and Lk 18:22.

They understood, once and for all, that Christ was their "place".

"They follow the Lamb wherever he goes."[22]

They are as if possessed by a passion for similarity.

Others offer their life, their family, their home, their work, in order to make themselves the work of incarnation inaugurated by Christ.

They ask that all of themselves be erased in order for Christ to clothe them with the life of man that he lived.

They ask that Christ incarnate himself in all the realities of their lives.

They ask to put on Christ and nothing else.

They receive a specific apostolic task: to save the people of this profession, or of that family, or of that social realm, and, in order to do this, to espouse in the extreme everything that will bring them closer to those they must save.

They believe that the remedy taken by Christ two thousand years ago should last until the end of time and that the little troupe, poor like him, pure like him, obedient like him, that he trained on the roads of Palestine must have traveled all the roads of the earth before the end of time.

This troupe must renew itself with each generation, with the Lord marking in advance those who will walk in his likeness.

[22] Rev 14:4.

From the first preaching of the Gospel, many people were disciples of Jesus Christ who stayed in their homes, and yet others had to leave their homes;

—many people peaceably kept possession of their goods, receiving the Lord at their table, and even providing him with grand hospitality;

—and yet others had to give away everything they had to the poor and run the race without support.

Both roads have always existed.

The Lord will always say to some:

"Because of me and for love of me you will have a wife, children, a house, goods to manage on my behalf in the world."

The Lord will always say to others:

"You will have nothing but me, and I will be your all."

The Lord will always say to some:

"I know what is right for you, I will give you your daily pain and your daily bread every day, so that everywhere you are there will also be my cross."

The Lord will always say to others "Take up your cross and follow me" . . . take it by the three arms of poverty, obedience, chastity. Why? Because this is how I want you to love me and how we will love the world together.

Most of those with whom Christ uses this language wear brown, white, or black robes, disciples of saints throughout the ages who were companions on the way of the Lord.

Others are people like you and me, people immersed as completely as possible in the thickness of the world, with no rule, vow, habit, or convent to separate them from this world—the same as people everywhere but poor, the same as people in any milieu but chaste; the same as people of any country, but obedient.

These people are made for everything and for everyone: among them you will find some who work in schools, others who write laws, some who care for and console people, others who work in a factory.

For them one world is as good as another and one soul as good as another soul.

But do not bother them with methods and techniques.

Do not tell them: "Here, it is better to appear somewhat wealthy: you will have more success", "Over there, it would be better to be married, you will be a better apostle", or: "Know what you want and stick to it."

They will reply to you: "We cannot take two roads. You are giving us recipes that are not meant for us.

"If we are a little shabby, if we look a bit like campers to the world, it is our own recipe, it is to possess only the Lord.

"If we do not have a household, if, at our house, neither husband nor wife nor child waits for us, it is because we belong to the Lord, and we want to belong to him alone.

"If we do not have a schedule, it is because it is our Father in Heaven wrote one for us in advance, and it is enough for us to receive his instructions from day to day."

Do not tell them that the cross is dangerous, a bit morbid, and very unhealthy, that the world needs to see the face of joy and not of penitence.

They will reply:

"We will speak to you of joy once we have found it on the cross where we find our love. Our joy comes at such an exorbitant cost that, in order to buy it, we had to sell what we possessed and our whole selves."

There must be many of those of the first calling, because the world is big and its baptism will take a long time.

But there must be at least a few of those of the second calling in order to provide men, these big children, with a visual representation of the life of Jesus: Jesus who is the "Mission" itself.

IV

The Essence of a Missionary

The Essence of Missionary Life

While the forms of missionary action are many, from fraternal shoulder-to-shoulder action to teaching, from teaching to practical mercy—while the two calls distinguish missionaries of two fraternal but different types —there is, however, a part of missionary life that is shared by all: this part is its essence.

The missionary is
someone who prays,
someone who gives witness,
someone who loves.

Voices That Pray in the Desert

Many of those [missionaries] who leave by boat end up in deserts in order to pray.

In these expanses without human footsteps, they feel at the heart of their task.

This silence is like the guarantee of their prayer, like the transmitter of their prayer to the door of all far-away hearts.

Solitude imparts them like an omnipresence amid all the lives they want to reach.

There, where there is no one, they speak truly on behalf of all.

There, where no human being breathes, they are alone as if in order to receive the weight of the presence, of the grace, of the Redemption of God.

The desert gives a man the magnitude of the Church.

We speak of a "Desert of Love". Love aspires to the Desert because the desert hands man over to God stripped of his country, his friendships, his fields, his home.

In the desert, man is dispossessed of what he loves, free from those who love him, submitted to God in a tremendous heart-to-heart.

That is why the spirit has always driven those who love into the Desert.

Missionaries without boats, propelled by the same love, the same spirit drives us toward other deserts.

From atop his sand dune, the missionary in white sees the expanse of unbaptized lands.

From the top of the long staircase of the subway, as missionaries in suits or raincoats, we see during rush hour, step by step, an expanse of heads, an agitated expanse waiting for the doors to open. Caps, berets, hats, hair of every color. Hundreds of heads: hundreds of souls.

We at the top.

And even higher up, and everywhere, God.

God everywhere, and how many souls know it?

God everywhere, we know well, except in most of these souls.

Later, when the doors open, we will climb into the subway car. We will see faces, foreheads, eyes, mouths. Mouths of people alone, by themselves: some miserly, others impure, others mean, mouths greedy or satisfied by all earthly foods, so few, so few that bear the shape of the Gospel.

Later again, when we arrive, in the dark, we will come out into the fresh air and go down the street that will bring us home.

Through the fog, the rain, or the moonlight, we will pass people: we will hear them talk about packages, bacon, money, promotions, fear, obstacles: never, or almost never, of that which is our love.

To the right, to the left, houses completely dark with little lines of light that tell us that in all this darkness there are living people.

We know well what they are doing: they are building their fragile joys; they are suffering their long miseries, they are doing a little good and sinning a lot.

How little light there would be if a small light shone
wherever a soul was praying.

Yes, we have our deserts . . . and love leads us there.

The same spirit that leads our brothers in white into
their own deserts, leads us, sometimes with heart racing, to rough stairways, in the subway, in dark streets.

We do not envy our brothers in white.

In this crowd, heart pressed to heart, squeezed between so many bodies, on our bench where three
strangers keep us company, in the dark street, our heart
quivers like a fist closed on a bird.

The Holy Spirit, all of the Holy Spirit in our poor
heart, the love great as God that beats in us, like a
sea that wants to break forth with all its strength, to
spread out and penetrate all these impermeable beings,
all these beings with no way out.

To be able to pace up and down all the streets, to
sit in all the subways, to climb all the stairs, to carry
the Lord God everywhere: here or there will be a soul
that has kept its human fragility in the face of God's
grace, a soul that has forgotten to harden itself with
gold or cement.

And then to pray, to pray as one prays in the middle
of other deserts, to pray for all these people, so close
to all, so close to God.

Desert of crowds. To dive into the crowd as into
the white sand.

Desert of crowds, desert of love.

Nakedness of real love. Let us not regret the loss of either the countryside or the friend who understood everything we had in our hearts, or the sweet hour in a corner of the church, or the cherished book back at home.

Desert where we are the prey of love.

This love that inhabits us, this love that bursts forth from us, shall it not shape us?

Lord, Lord, at least let this rind that covers me not be a barrier to you. Pass through.

My eyes, my hands, my mouth are yours.

This woman so sad before me: here is my mouth so that you can smile at her.

This child is almost gray, he is so pale: here are my eyes so that you can look upon him.

This man so tired, so very tired, here is my whole body so that you can give him my seat, and my voice so that you can say very gently to him: "Sit down." This boy, so smug, so foolish, so tough, here is my heart for you to love him with, harder than he has ever been loved.

Missions to the desert, missions without fail, sure missions, missions where we sow God in the middle of the world, confident that he will germinate somewhere because:

"Where there is no love, put love, and you will reap love."

Witnesses

We do not take the word of God to the ends of the earth in a suitcase: we carry it in us, we take it in us.

We do not put it in a corner of ourselves, in our memory, as on a closet shelf where we keep it in storage. We let it go to the depths of ourselves, to that hinge on which our whole-selves pivot.

We cannot be missionaries without having made this frank, wide, cordial welcome in ourselves to the word of God, to the Gospel.

The living tendency of this word is to become flesh, to become flesh in us.

And when we are thus inhabited by it, we become fit to be missionaries.

But let us make no mistake. We know that it is very costly to receive the message intact within us. That is why so many of us retouch it, mutilate it, mitigate it.

We feel the need to make him fashionable, as if God were not always fashionable, as if we were touching up God.

If the missionary priest is the spokesman for the Word of God, we missionaries without the priesthood are a kind of sacrament.

Once we have experienced the Word of God, we do not have the right not to receive it; once we have received it, we do not have the right not to allow it to become flesh in us; once it has become flesh in us, we do not have the right to keep it for ourselves: from then on, we belong to those who await it.

The time of martyrs comes and goes, but the time of witnesses goes on endlessly, and witnesses means martyrs.

This incarnation of the Word of God in us, this docility of allowing ourselves to be molded by it— this is what we call witnessing.

If our witness is often so mediocre, it is because we do not realize that being a witness requires the same heroism as being a martyr.

In order to take the Word of God seriously, we need all the strength of the Holy Spirit in us.

"To live today as if this evening I should die a martyr", wrote Father de Foucauld.

"To begin this hour knowing that it will be necessary to be a martyr, to be a witness", we could say at the beginning of every hour of our days, because there is no hour in which we have the right to allow the Word of God to fall asleep in us. And this implies a fervor of our whole selves in the face of the grace of every moment, a desperate longing for this strength without which we would be renegades.

A missionary I know, who believes in the Word of God, gave to a woman who did not believe some pages of the Word of God to type up, certain that this would put her in contact with the Lord. That woman converted.

Let us have this faith and this simplicity. Let us allow ourselves to be increasingly inhabited by the word, and as we, in turn, dwell among our brothers, let us believe that this proximity will draw them closer to their God.

People Who Love

". . . As I have loved you".[23]

This is not advice; it is not up for choosing.

For the two thousand years that we have been trying to obey Jesus Christ, we have made such a catalogue of virtues that we no longer really know how to distinguish the essential from the accidental.

Poverty, justice, honesty, obedience . . . and all the rest. Yes, of course . . . "but [if I] have not love, I gain nothing".[24]

We must love with that charity that is not man-made, with that charity that is divine.

And what a caricature we have already made of it: philanthropy, altruism, solidarity . . .

Charity is only learned in the heart of Christ and in the Charter of his heart that is the Gospel.

We have made distinctions that we were not asked to make. On the one hand, the commandments that we agree with in principle: "You shall not kill, you shall not steal . . ."[25] On the other hand, those we consider exaggerated in practice: "and if anyone would sue you

[23] Jn 13:34.
[24] 1 Cor 13:3.
[25] Ex 20.

and take your coat, let him have your cloak as well'',[26]
. . . turn the other cheek when they strike the first,
serve those who demand service from you, treat as
God's children those who mistreat and mock you.

To love in this way would be truly scandalous because we are not used to it.

And even when we have received this lesson from
the heart of Christ, when we have set our own hearts
in the right direction, it remains for us to knock down
the good manners accepted as proper in the world, it
remains for us to make a beautiful scandal of charity.

Consider this. Let us take a very small piece of our
life and set free the charity of Christ in it to see everything it can do, everything it wants to do, and to let
it do it.

You change trains, you wait in the waiting room in
the middle of the night. The charity of the Lord is in
you in the midst of this waiting room. What is it going
to do? What will that very polite lady, this very proper
gentleman, say when you share coffee from your ther-
mos with the neighbor to your right, your bread and
your cheese with the neighbor to your left, if you wrap
that child in your coat . . . But what will Christ say if
you do not do it?

The holy Church expects saints, and saints are those
who love.

The holy Church holds her great heart in her hands,
the heart of Our Lord Jesus Christ.

[26] Mt 5:40.

Who will be willing to receive it?

Who will be willing to love it?

But that is not all.

There is also the other side of the sole commandment: "You shall love the LORD your God . . .

[and you shall love him] with all your heart, and with all your soul,

and with all your might."[27]

When people believe in God, we think everything is fine. And yet, God did not say: "You shall believe", but "You shall love." To the people he has made supernaturally alive through Faith, he gives only one commandment, which is to love, and to love with all that is ourselves and to love him above all.

God did not say, "You John, you Peter, you Madeleine, you shall love because you are someone exceptional and because your love will especially please me." God said to the whole world: "The first and greatest commandment is this: You shall love the Lord your God . . ."

It is to everyone, to all people, that this has been said.

And it is through understanding this that missionaries are made.

Understanding that we must love God, even like a madman—this can make people virtuous.

But to understand that God wants all this love, the love of all men who were born, who are born, or who will be born: it is this that makes Missionaries.

[27] Dt 6:5.

"Love is not being loved", cry the missionaries of every time and every kind.

It consoles them very little to have a touch of God's love in their heart if the multitudes remain icy before "a thing so good it could not be better".[28]

If they knew that God wants only themselves, no doubt their poor love would suffice: but God wants the world, and what would they not do in order to give it to him.

Saint Thérèse of the Child Jesus, patroness of missionaries, said: "In the heart of the Church, my Mother, I will be love." And she explains in a lyrical fashion, which we would gladly call romantic, how we can, within the Church, produce love.

This page, read and reread by those who love Saint Thérèse as well as by those who have little love for her, is not actually taken seriously in all its profound truth. What she wanted to tell us, what she lived, what brought about such stunning results in her life, is that to love produces love in the Church. It is that within the unbreakable unity of the Church, those who love pour forth, according to the measure of their love, so to speak, a pure charity. Charity is to the Church what blood is to our heart. "I understood that she had a

[28] This is how Lord de Joinville replied to his king, Saint Louis, who asked him: "Senechal, what is God?" (cf. *Le Livre des saintes paroles et des bons faits de notre saint roi Louis*, by Jean de Joinville, chap. IV: "How the king hated sin, and what love he had for the poor").

heart'', Saint Thérèse again tells us. To love is to be the heart of the Church; it is to send blood to the farthest away, to the most anemic of her members.

But make no mistake: this lesson of love is not a rose-scented lesson, even though it is given by the saint of roses.

To love is not to tremble or be emotional: this much we have already been made to understand. But neither is to love merely to do one's duty: and this is less known.

Three working women can be sewing together, all with the same submission to the will of God: it will not be with the same love.

We love when the will submits itself, but also when it desires with all its strength, as the best of goods, as the only good that it wants, the thing that at this moment God gives it to do, to enjoy, or to suffer.

With love, there is a whole scale of intensity, and this intensity is measured by our joy.

But this love belongs only to those who are free, to those who are free from themselves, who have come out of themselves once and for all.

We do not love as much when we remain barracked within ourselves.

Saint Thérèse of the Child Jesus also called herself ''of the Holy Face'', and that is no accident for this missionary.

It is because, in fact, the saint of the Face of Jesus Christ is the sovereign mistress of coming out of oneself.

To the missionary, to the man folded in on himself, God commands this essential conversion of leaving himself, of unfolding himself.

This is the price of love.

Saint Francis of Assisi truly began to love on the day when, hanging from the rotting neck of a leper, he embraced the thing he feared most in the world with his own lips.

No love is possible outside the cross, and it is because God wants us to love him that he gives us the right to suffer.

Whether missionaries have been called to one or the other of these two roads, they are all called to the cross, whether God gives it to them or they take it.

There are not small or large crosses: there is simply the cross that we receive this morning, this evening, tomorrow, the day after tomorrow, a small or large piece.

It is the cross hidden in a telephone call that keeps us from acknowledging it, the cross hidden in our pen that delays our correspondence, the cross hidden in our work that makes us afraid of Monday, the cross hidden in life that makes us bored, the cross found in death that makes us cry.

"Love everything you have burned", cry all the saints from above every baptism, "if you want to be free to love."

And this love that God commands we give him, as suffusive in us as the blood in our veins, is the clearest of our missionary work.

Because through our own task, we work on souls for whom grace, ultimately, will be decisive. But through love we put into action the universal and indispensable act of the Church.

Because, as Saint Thérèse always tells us, "It is love that makes missionaries", and it is love that makes converts as well.

Our Lady of the Missions

Holy Mary, you who know, better than anyone, that every mission is the continuation of the redemptive Incarnation of your son, give to us, missionaries of our poor time, the authentic meaning of this Incarnation and redemption.

Let us descend into the depths of this world, to take there the Word of God lived with all the strength of our heart.

Let us understand that to pursue this Incarnation is not to remake grace in the image of the world but to infuse the world with a life so powerful and new that it is revivified and rejuvenated.

Let us not reduce Christ to the size of the world, but raise the world up to the size of Jesus Christ.

Make us understand that the second phase of the Incarnation is the return to God of a world to which God has come.

"God made himself man, so that man may be made God."[29]

Teach us to "establish all things in Christ",[30] and him crucified, you in whom the Incarnation began, for you were the first and fully redeemed.

Teach us not to believe in recipes for happiness other than the beatitudes, not to want to bring to our pagans a Messiah that Christ did not want to be, an opulent and idolized Messiah.

You who held in your arms the baby of the manger and the dead one of Calvary, protect us from every illusion that would make us blush at his poverty and his Cross.

But above all, holy Mary, Mother of God, be our capacity for grace, the silence where the word of God, without modification and without distortion, will be able to take possession of us, the docility where the Holy Spirit will form the Missionary that we should be.

Feast of Saint John the Evangelist

1943

---

[29] Irenaeus, *Adversus haereses* (Against heresies) III, 10, 2, and V, Pr., reprised by several Church Fathers, including Saint Athanasius and Saint Leo the Great.

[30] Eph 1:10 translation from the Vulgate: "Omnia instaurare in Christo".

Why We Love Father de Foucauld
(1946)

This text about Charles de Foucauld was published by Madeleine Delbrêl in the review *La Vie spirituelle* in November 1946. It demonstrates a long acquaintance with the life and thought of the one she calls "the saint of the desert". Mindful of what is published by him and about him, she begins her article by referencing the "testament" of Venerable Little Sister Magdeleine of Jesus published in the April 1946 issue of *La Vie spirituelle*, as well as a text by Charles de Foucauld about apostolates in lay life published in the same review in April 1930.

What documents were available to her in 1946? Of course, the first large biography, that of René Bazin published by Plon in 1921; to this we must add that of Georges Gorrée, *Sur les traces de Charles de Foucauld* (In the footsteps of Charles de Foucauld), published by La Plus Grande France in 1936, which had been preceded by a work by Paul Lesourd published by Flammarion in 1933: *La Vraie figure de Charles de Foucauld* (The true face of Charles de Foucauld). As for de Foucauld's writings, she was familiar with two essential works: *Écrits spirituels* (The spiritual writings), published by René Bazin for Gigord in 1923, and Letters à Henri de Castries, published by Grasset in 1938, which Madeleine cites extensively in her article.

Charles de Foucauld clearly played an important role in the spiritual formation of Madeleine's group the Charity. From 1931, in a report from a group meeting, we find this surprising expression: the group "is less animated by a very active missionary spirit than by a desire to live like de Foucauld. No longer 'to work for Christ', but 'to be Christ in order to do what Christ does'.[1] In this quote, we see that the Charity of Jesus (it is hard not to draw a parallel with Jesus Caritas) aligned itself early on with the school of Charles de Foucauld. Under whose influence? That of Abbot Lorenzo, no doubt, whose personal vocation certainly found support and confirmation in "the saint of the desert". Whatever it was, it did not come from Madeleine alone but rather from the whole group, which was confirmed fifteen years later by the very title that Madeleine gave her article: "Why We Love Father de Foucauld".

Various experts on Charles de Foucauld say that Madeleine understood his spiritual thought perfectly. It is not necessary to summarize here what the reader will discover in these pages. If the reader is familiar with Madeleine, he will find several major themes of Madeleine's spiritual personality here: the theocentrism expressed in adoration, the unconditional love

---

[1] Madeleine Delbrêl archives: *Madeleine Delbrêl. Genèse d'une spiritualité* (Paris: Nouvelle Cité, 2008), 57.

of neighbor, whoever he may be, the central place of the mystery of the Cross, and the fundamental role of the Eucharist. This is how much she was affected by "the saint of the desert".

It is easy to see how Madeleine dramatizes the death of Father de Foucauld by saying his body was discovered a month after his death. This is refuted by the facts. In reality, after the departure of his assassins, the body of Father de Foucauld was buried by the inhabitants of Douar, who gave him his initial grave. Why does Madeleine deviate from history in this way? It is because she wants to draw a parallel between the body of Charles de Foucauld and the Eucharistic body of Christ, itself thrown on the ground (not outside as she says, but in the chapel). In her interpretation of the death of Father, she sees him identified with the Eucharistic Christ, handed over to men—so much so that in this perspective, we find at the end of Madeleine's article the summit of her missionary thought: Charles de Foucauld revealed himself as an apostle to the inhabitants of the desert, no matter who they were, allowing the Word to transform him internally by a permanent conversion, as the account of the group cited above says: "to be Christ in order to do what Christ does". Identified in this way with Christ by conversion in obedience to the Word, the apostle goes the whole way in this identification with the Eucharistic mystery. It is a matter of being Christ to the end, delivered to men in his sacrifice.

Lastly, let us note that in the first edition of this text

published in 1968 in *La Joie de croire* (*The Joy of Believing*), the whole passage on the Eucharist was omitted. The goal of the editors of *We, the Ordinary People of the Streets* and *The Joy of Believing* was to publish excerpts from the writings of Madeleine in order to introduce her thought. So they had to abridge the texts. It was necessary for this text to be published now in its entirety in order to restore balance both to the thought of Charles de Foucauld and to that of Madeleine Delbrêl.

Curiously, this article was signed "D. M." Although Madeleine Delbrêl published a good number of articles in this period of her life, she retained a certain anonymity.

We are republishing the text published in *La Vie spirituelle*.

~

[From the editors of *La Vie spirituelle*]: *The "Testament" of Mother Magdeleine of Jesus was published in the April issue of this review. It brought us a message from the official and direct lineage of Father de Foucauld.*

Around the same time, by chance, we discovered in La Vie spirituelle *from April 1930 a letter by Father [de Foucauld] about lay apostolates. This letter highlights the considerable influence that the "saint of the Desert" had on the climate of our times and how, recognized or not, his influence affected a good number of contemporary vocations. The extensive summary of his life explains how such dissimilar paths can lay claim to him. He alone combines so many contrasts.*

An uncontrollable need to pray before God, an immeasurable gift to anyone who asks for it.

An ingenuous imitation of Christ's life in Palestine, of his deeds, of his actions.

A knowledge of and adaptation to his surroundings.

A passionate love of neighbor. A faithful love for all of humanity at every moment.

Such a tender reestablishment of the house of Nazareth around an exposed Host; "taming" hikes across Saharan trails.

Heroic perseverance in a harshly outlined vocation; comprehension of and preparation for the vocation of others.

Devotion to the work manually *accomplished*, tireless perseverance in a labor of learning.

Relentless desire for a spiritual family with three branches, divine vocation to a solitude of which his death will be the consummation.

How can we be surprised that in this intersection of graces that was this life, so many of those who presently give themselves to God, whatever the mode of this gift may be, recognize their call and find a model?

Also, leaving to others the opportunity to say what in Father de Foucauld enlightened, guided, or confirmed them on their path, we wish simply to highlight here the aspects of his life that helped us to find ours.

"In Pure Loss of Oneself"

To rise before God in pure loss of oneself, says Charles de Foucauld, quoting Bossuet.

From his whole life there emerges an extraordinary character of freeness. God, if he is his God, always remains God, and it is first and foremost because he is God that Charles de Foucauld loves him.

For him, prayer will never dispense him from adoration. "Pure adoration", we read in one of his schedules, and, further on, "pure prayer"—and this shows that these are two different things for him. Likewise, gratitude does not dispense him from admiration: he admires Jesus because he is Jesus.

He is a kind of ordinary ecstatic who, once and for all, took up residence outside of himself. It suffices as the purpose of his life to be positioned somewhere, the farthest away possible, among unbelievers in order to adore God and his Son Jesus Christ.

> How you understand adoration, my very dear friend [he wrote to H. de Castries], and with what compelling feeling you see that adoration—which is the most complete expression of perfect love—is the act par excellence, but his habitual action and even his continual action, if he acts in accordance with his nature and his reason . . . gives thanks to God for his great glory, as you say so well, in an admiration, a contemplation, an adoration, a respect, a love with-

out end; it is the end for which we are made, it will
be our life in heaven, and it is our life in this world if
we act as rational beings. It is clear that, compared to
God, all creation is nothing, and when we can give
all thought, all love, all heart, all spirit to the All, how
can we let the least part of it go astray and lose itself in
nothingness. . . . We love all men, however, and we
love them to the point of giving each of them our life
whole-heartedly, but it is because of God who loves
them paternally that we love them too, as we love the
children of a passionately beloved person. . . .

In the end, the foundation of love, of adoration,
is to lose oneself, is to perish into what we love and
regard all the rest as nothing: Islam does not have
enough contempt for creatures in order to be able to
teach a love of God worthy of God: without chastity
and poverty, love and adoration remain always very
imperfect because when we love passionately we separate ourselves from everything that can distract, if
only for a minute, from the beloved, and we throw
ourselves into and lose ourselves completely in him.
(*Lettres à H. de C.*, p. 89)

For us he is the type of theocentric vocation that
captures the soul directly for God in Christ. These
men do not have a choice to make. God touches the
whole horizon. By the very fact that he exists, he is
eminently preferred. "As soon as I believed there was a
God, I understood that I could not do otherwise than
to live only for him: my religious vocation dates from
the same hour as my faith: God is so great, there is

such a difference between God and everything that is not him" (*Lettres à H. de C.*, p. 97).

For these men, the love of Jesus Christ leads to the love of all our brothers, as for others the vocation to the apostolate will be the path of a total gift to Christ.

Indeed this gratitude vis-à-vis God is found vis-à-vis his neighbor. Charles de Foucauld gives his neighbor his life every day, and we know that with that greatness of gift and availability, he is ready to die for him—and he did die by and for him. He does not await the results, is not troubled by his complete failure, maintains his peace when, having spent almost his whole life in the desert, his only accomplishment is the conversions, not even guaranteed, of a black man and an old woman. He loves for love's sake because God is love, and because God is in him, and in loving all his creatures "to the end", he imitates his Lord as much as possible.

Because as a man of adoration, Father de Foucauld was a man of solitude and of the desert. Wherever a man goes, there is his desert: man must make his desert.

In Beni Abbès, he wrote the following:

You must break everything that is not me . . . to make yourself a desert here where you are as alone with me as Magdeleine was alone in the Desert with me. It is through detachment that you will achieve this, in chasing away all these little thoughts, all these infinitely little things that are not bad in and of themselves but that end by dispersing your spirit from morning to evening far from me, whereas, from morning to evening you should be contemplating me.

Father de Foucauld truly illuminated God's first commandment to humanity for us with new clarity: "You shall have no other gods before me . . ."

Prayer has often been compared to a breath. Through the writings of Father, adoration is explained as the "weight" of the soul, as that which places it before its God in its human attitude. This attitude of the creature vis-à-vis his creator: we think it is the right one for us to adopt, and urgently, in our world that is inverted toward man, diverted from its end. It is essential that many of us devote ourselves to it. It is like a need of the mystical body in this moment when the Holy Spirit drives so many vocations toward the pursuit of lost men, when so many Christians, urged by the charity of Christ, desperately search for those who are lost in order to do everything for everyone—apart from sin—in order to go seek them at the extreme limits of their separation and their bewilderment. We need others turned toward God. We believe that even inside the human mass of dough, we need men of adoration, so convinced of the necessity of their task that, even deprived of any action toward their fellow beings, even without knowing the precise needs of their brothers, they would know that they respond to the essence of their vocation in repeating to God in our contemporary deserts: on our subways and in our streets, in our homes and on our farms: "You are the one who is; we are those who are not."

Our time needs these "sacrifices" accomplished among men who are unaware of them. It needs "crosses that cry out in our deserts", that phrase with which the writings of Father de Foucauld abound and which was an axis for his life: "We give you thanks for your great glory", "in pure loss of ourselves".

The Universal Brother

Father de Foucauld seems to us rooted at the crossroads of charity. He does not refuse any of the approaches to love. He welds the two extremes of love together in his life: love of neighbor and of the whole world.

To be a "gentle brother", he often says; and this word "gentle" continually returns laden with human solicitude; to be a "savior", he also says, and this word carries the whole weight of redemption.

In his life, he fully combines the vocation to go about "doing good" and to redeem from within.

To the word "caritas", written so often above the heart and the cross, he gives full meaning in depth and extent. He deliberately settles into family life with every human being he meets. And this family life, truly lived, will be the necessary sign of another family life continuously deepened by day and by night with all the men of the earth.

Living this double family life will mean having only rocks piled in the sand for a cloister; it will mean listening much and speaking little; it will mean giving his ration of food or a lesson in knitting; bringing a Tuareg chief to France and going all the way to Tamanrasset; collecting local poems and taking care [of people]; living alone among Muslims and dying alone, killed by them. It will mean giving to each person what he needs because Jesus is essentially the one who gives and because Charles of Jesus acts with him and as him. It will mean not having a plan specifying what one can and cannot do. It will mean being for each person what his "gentle brother" would be. It will mean seeing sinners as "foolish brothers" and reserving for them the warmest affection of his heart. And all in giving himself up with an unreserved generosity to the men who surround him, not allowing himself to be annexed by them. Knowing that through them, charity bursts forth and explodes in the world, preparing for grace.

"Lord, make all human beings go to heaven", he planned to teach as a first prayer to the catechumens he would never have. All the prayers, all the penance of the Rule of the Little Brothers of the Sacred Heart were directed toward the intentions of the Sovereign Pontiff—that is to say, on the very scale of the world.

From Father de Foucauld we have learned that, while to give oneself to the whole world, one must be willing to break away from all mooring in order to be "cast adrift on the sea", it is not necessary for this sea to be contained between the walls of a monastery. It can fit in an enclosure of dry rocks placed directly on the sand; it can fit within an African caravan; it can fit in one of our homes, in a workshop, in a stairway that we climb, in a bus that we take. We find the wide by accepting the narrow, the constant enclosure of the love of the close neighbor. To give to each of those whom we approach the entirety of perfect charity, to allow oneself to be chained by this incessant and all-consuming dependence, to live the Sermon on the Mount naturally—this is the sea gate, the narrow gate that leads to universal charity.

He taught us how to be perfectly content to be placed at a crossroads of life, ready to love whoever passes, and, through him, all who are suffering in the world, lost or in darkness.

He explained to us that in his magnificent selflessness is to be found sovereign efficiency and that to consent not to see anything that we do, but to love nonetheless and forever, is the best path for saving someone, somewhere, on the earth.

A Heart Planted with a Cross

The heart planted with a cross taught us that this total charity is only possible at the cost of all the negatives that are, so to speak, its other side: poverty, obedience, purity, humility . . . all these negatives that "make one free to love". Also at the cost of what might be called negative, but that is positive and better, the voluntary cross, participation in the Passion of the Lord, whether that means pain for the body or the soul, suffering or humiliation, or, in the words of Charles de Foucauld, desired *abjection*. In this realm, the heart planted with a cross also teaches us that all the reasons of reason are worth little in the face of the reasons of the heart.

> Penitence . . . : you do not need to see its beauty. Does it not suffice for you to know that I did it all my life, that I practiced it all my hidden life . . . does not this example suffice for you to enter with all your strength into penitence without any other reason, by pure love and simple need to imitate me, to resemble me, to share my life and especially my pains?

This cross is truly the axis of his heart, the solid pivot around which his universal love will orient itself.

The message that we have received from him is the necessity of this axis. Without it, our charity will remain indefinitely anemic, incomplete, mutilated. Charity that does not bear the cross within it constantly runs into other crosses—it stumbles, it crawls. Charity that is connected to the cross has overcome the obstacle in advance.

"Jesus-Caritas" is written above and below this heart and cross. It is because love without suffering remains our own love; saving love, the love of Jesus, is a love that suffers, and it is through suffering, through the perceptible good, that it accomplishes redemption. The heart planted with a cross is a heart that wants to suffer. It goes farther than the suffering that comes by itself, farther than the suffering connected to all that is poverty, humility, obedience. It goes all the way to desired suffering.

> When we can suffer and love, we can do much, we can do the most that we can in this world.

These words are Father de Foucauld's; he wrote them on December 1, 1916, the day of his death. They are a response to that which in our time still speaks of the scandal of the Cross and blushes at a Christianity in which it is necessary to suffer and to count for little.

To Proclaim the Gospel by My Life

"A violent desire for imitation", Father de Foucauld says somewhere. He often repeats that we cannot love without admiring, and that we cannot admire without imitating.

"Your vocation", he wrote: "to preach the Gospel in silence. . . . Your rule, to follow me. . . . To do what I would do. Ask yourself in everything, 'What would our Lord have done?' and do that. That is your only rule, but it is your absolute rule."

He is truly, in the mid-twentieth century, a genuine contemporary of Jesus of Nazareth. He follows him by way of a rustic and meticulous imitation. He contemplates him by placing himself deliberately in the midst of the apostles "between the Blessed Mother and Saint Magdalene". He wants to become one of the friends of the Master, he blends into their life, he listens, all ears, to the teachings of the Lord, going over all of his words with a fine-tooth comb in order to obey them up to the final point. It is this imitation that is never satisfied that will lead him to the priesthood.

By looking at him, at Charles de Foucauld, we learn this childlike obedience to the Gospel message, this confident obedience that does not ask for an explanation, that obeys, not because of what is ordered, but because of who orders it.

The Gospel is for him the entirety of his visible apostolate. He gives his brothers an illustrated edition of this Gospel, thinking these images of life are the better conveyance of grace. In seeing him embody every line of the "good news", we have understood what men need, which is to read and to see at the same time. The Apostles preached and lived their message, and their whole message: the beatitude of poverty along with the rest of it. Is it not from the dissociation of preaching and life, of the word and example, that lack of contagion arises?

From this evangelic life, all the strength of simplicity has also emerged for us. It has shown us a possible human and Christian state of mind in which we find ourselves on equal footing with every person we meet. Father de Foucauld resurrected for us the figure, brotherly to all, of Jesus in Palestine, welcoming into his heart, according to their paths, workers and scholars, Jews and foreigners, the sick and children, as simple as he was, understandable to all.

He teaches us that, alongside necessary apostolates where the apostle must clothe himself with the environment of those he wants to evangelize, and almost espouse it, there is another apostolate that demands a simplification of one's whole being, a rejection of all prior gain, of all our social selves, a rather dizzying poverty. This kind of evangelic or apostolic poverty makes us totally agile so that we can join any one of our brothers, on any terrain, without any innate or acquired baggage that prevents us from running toward him.

Alongside the specialized apostolate, he poses the question of being everything to all.

He who in the heart of the desert, buried within Muslim communities, was the friend of every passerby, soldier, teacher, doctor—he who knew how to engage so completely with the "tours" of someone like Laperrine[2]—he elevates us above social compartments, below human groups, so that we might become a universal message readable by all.

God with Us

When, almost a month after his assassination, they found the body of Father de Foucauld "stripped of everything, stretched on the ground . . . unrecognizable, covered with blood and wounds, violently and painfully killed", the monstrance was lying with him on the same sand, and, in the monstrance, the Host,

[2] Commandant François Laperrine, friend of Charles de Foucauld. He was named superior commandant of the Saharan Oasis in 1901.

the body of Our Lord. It was like a demonstration of similarity.

We do not know if a complete reading of the writings of Father de Foucauld would give the same impression, but what we have been able to read of them shows that his missionary vocation was connected to a Eucharistic vocation.

In weighing his reasons for accepting the priesthood, did he not say: "Here, I could do infinitely more for neighbor, by the sole offering of the Holy Sacrifice, by the establishment of a tabernacle that, through the sole presence of the Blessed Sacrament, will invisibly sanctify the surroundings as Our Lord, in the bosom of his mother, sanctified the house of John"?

It seems that this vocation connects the Father with the same impetus of Our Lord's desire to dwell upon the whole earth. It seems that it makes him free to be completely available to the Blessed Sacrament, an immense Yes to sacramental grace.

This monk, lying at the foot of the tabernacle or carrying the Host along desert trails or constantly going farther so that the sacrifice of the Mass could be offered farther away, and so that Christ could constantly be in residence farther away—this monk seems to be offered like prey, like a dough perfectly malleable and supple for receiving the grace of the Eucharist.

It seems that Charles de Foucauld in this whole final part of his life had the unique mission of expressing, by the sign of his life, the mysterious sign of the Blessed Sacrament. It was as if he was welded to, connected to, the Host in order to be made by it into someone immolated and praying, delivered to men to be eaten by them, someone simple to the extreme, perfectly digestible, perfectly edible. A man eaten, constantly linked to God, food eaten by his constant service to his brothers, who became prayer and immolation with this very God.

Better than anyone, Father de Foucauld was aware of the abysses of grace potentially contained in a tabernacle, but for which a link with the world is necessary, for which dedicated people are necessary, who are like the common thread, like the power outlet, like the connection to all poor humanity. And these men are better conductors of grace to the extent that they agree to reproduce in themselves the essential evangelic message that Our Lord preaches to them in the Eucharist.

If there were such electric shocks of grace from the heart of the Sahara, if such waves of charity were set in motion to such an extent that we still perceive them moving among us, it is because a human being fully accepted possession by Christ in his tabernacle, to live only as a function of him, to be, so to speak, the transmitter of his mercy.

If, on the contrary, so many tabernacles of our cities, of our organizations, of our villages seem like sepulchers of a loved one, it is because they lack people prostrated before them whose sole occupation is to receive from the Eucharist the grace that will make them prayerful, immolated, and given to their brothers.

Everywhere that there were adorers in the churches "in spirit and in truth"—a Curé d'Ars, a Benedict Labre, a Charles de Foucauld—grace shook up souls and the world trembled.

Here again Father de Foucauld made himself a teacher. If what is needed, in this moment, among our brothers, are souls obsessed by the trenches that have been dug between the pagans and us, what is also needed are souls obsessed by the lack of "welding" between the tabernacle and Christians: without these souls, the chain of grace will be missing links.

Do we understand sufficiently, at the present time, that one of the underlying reasons for the existence of parishes is to allow Christians to huddle together near the "God with us"? Do not our parishes lack this secret energy that would spark the expansion of grace because they lack this ardent recourse to Christ present among his own?

We are astonished, and rightly so, at how much time is devoted by parish communities to their own sanctification when so many unbelievers suffer around them. Could we not be, again even more rightly, astonished at how little time is dedicated by these same Christians to the company of Christ? It is Father de Foucauld who triggered this astonishment about our own lives.

The Last Place

"Christ took the last place so often that no one was ever able to take it from him."

It is with these words of Abbot Huvelin[3] "indelibly carved into the soul" of Father de Foucauld that we will end this evocation of him.

He understood with all his being—and he helps us to understand—that real intimacy with Christ happens if we join him in the place that is his: the last. He helped us to lose faith in prestige and to acquire faith in our own disappearance. He purified our idea of testimony of any tendency to "billboard advertising", according to the phrase of a priest who understood him well. He taught us that, while some are called to hold, in the spirit of Christ, the reins of temporal things or charitable responsibilities, others are called to bury themselves in the last place with Christ for the simple purpose of sharing it with him. On the front of *La Modèle unique* (The only model), the small book in which only phrases from the Gospel are written, Father de Foucauld placed the image of the Holy Face: the Christ of insults, derisions, abandonments, and failures. It is the last of last places. *Sicut Deus dilexi*

[3] Abbot Henri Huvelin (1838–1910), then vicar of the Parish of Saint-Augustin in Paris, exercised a decisive influence on Charles de Foucauld at the time of his conversion. He became his spiritual director.

nos,[4] he wrote as an inscription. "This is how God wants us to love him", responds the whole life of Charles of Jesus.

D. M.

[4] "As God has loved us."

Talk on Father de Foucauld (1950)

This second text about Charles de Foucauld is a talk given by Madeleine Delbrêl in Rambouillet in March 1950.[1] Here she lays out the life of Charles de Foucauld in its different segments and, at the same time, under the different aspects according to which he progressively came to identify himself with Christ. We will notice the same reflection on the configuration of the Eucharistic Christ given up for men that Madeleine developed in the previous text.

This comes from her lecture notes, which remained unfinished.

~

Father de Foucauld is
    a convert
    a man who encountered God
    a man who loved Christ
    a man who imitated him.
  This imitation
    led him to a life
    that did not want to reject

[1] According to the testimony of Christine de Boismarmin.

either prayer
or universal charity
or the mission
or the love of the world.
He was the man of God
living among men.
He configured himself to the Eucharist
little
God
among men
eaten by men.
He took on the life of Christ.
Christ gave him his death.

The convert is a man who discovers the marvelous good fortune that God exists.

He knew the vertigo of the absurd in an incoherent world; the unacceptability of a morality that is not mysticism, the bite of every day that is but a march toward death[2] . . .

And in a world that suddenly makes sense, in a moral life whose every demand is an expression of love, in the days that are a conveyance to eternity, explodes the certainty of God; "not of the God of philosophers and scholars", but of a living God, who jostles the hierarchy of values, the notion of joys, and who demands a passion too great for the greatest of human hearts.

---

[2] Madeleine Delbrêl had put a comma here, leaving the sentence in suspense. We replaced the comma with an ellipsis to reestablish movement in it.

From this central fact of a personal love with a personal God ensue, abruptly and in perfect order, all the demands of prayer, asceticism, charity, discipleship.

This sensational convert becomes like the visible brother of all those shattered by the grace that we now encounter.

But here he gives us his first lesson that has reverberated in so many lives.

He forces us to establish a parallel between the habituated believer and the convert.

He forces us to revise the order of the aspects of our life.

To ask ourselves if, too often, we do not only retain from our Christian life requirements that are cultural for some, moral for others, apostolic for others.

If reason makes these demands a burden in our life or an activity that utterly consumes us, is it not because we have eluded the central problem of this Christian life? Our personal encounter with the living God, an encounter that might be slow and patient—have we not learned what Father de Foucauld said: "God is so great and there is such a difference between God and everything that is not him"?

Adoration

The God whom Father de Foucauld encountered at that Mass of Saint-Augustin[3] is Jesus Christ.

---

[3] Reference to the parish of Saint-Augustin in the eighth arrondissement of Paris, where Charles de Foucauld had his conversion.

For him, the Love of Jesus Christ was an imitation.

"I do not understand love without a vehement desire for imitation."

This imitation made him first and foremost an adorer of God.

He surrendered himself to that same spirit of prayer that shows us Christ adoring and interceding in the Gospel.

This spirit led him to La Trappe Abbey, where he stayed for ten years.

But, "The vehement desire for imitation" was unsatisfied.

Jesus had been the Poor One and the one who exalts poverty.

La Trappe Abbey did not give him the concrete poverty and insecurity that his love demanded.

Jesus had been the little one, the one who had said, "What is exalted among men is an abomination in the sight of God."

In a sermon, a sentence had hit him right in the heart: "Jesus took the last place so often that no one was able to take it from him."[4]

This is why Brother Charles set out as a poor one among the poor for the land of the one whom he loved.

In shabby attire, he arrived in the town of the hidden life, Nazareth.

The Poor Clares housed him in a shed in their garden, and he became their handyman.

[4] A sermon by Abbot Huvelin at the time of Charles de Foucauld's conversion.

Praying, poor, and humble, he thought he would carry out his life there.

In the country of the unknown Christ, prostrated before the Eucharistic Christ, he thought he had found the place of his vocation.

But Christ had been a Priest, and he needed priests in order to continue to dwell among men.

But Christ came for the most lost among men, "and the vehement desire for imitation" began to push Brother Charles toward frontiers where the Gospel needed to go.

Driven by this restless desire, he returned to France, became a priest, and departed for the Sahara.

At Beni Abbès, he installed the Blessed Sacrament, he prayed, he kept vigil.[5]

But the love that dwelled in him continued to knead him from the inside, and it configured him to the one upon whom he gazed for hours and hours. It made him the sacrament of the people around him.

He conformed to the image of a compassionate, healing, consoling Jesus.

He became the brother, and through the near neighbor who visited him, he became the universal brother whose heart beat with [the heart] of Jesus Christ for the whole world.

Here again, he thought he had found the end of his unpredictable road. But again, love gave the signal for departure.

[5] Crossed out: ". . . he accepts . . ."

Laperrine suggested he depart for Hoggar, to the Tuareg people, the farthest away, the most lost.

Brother Charles, seeing Christ wandering the roads, places his feet in his footsteps and sets off.

After a few trips, love chose for him to settle in the midst of that people.

To settle in that extremity of the world.

This meant that for months, he would be without Mass, without Hosts. That he himself would be the presence of the Savior among the most lost of his flock.

The heart of Christ had so grown within him that his own form of sanctity burst forth, so that he himself no longer counted—like the Host at Mass, which, after having been offered and consecrated, has no other destiny than to be eaten, hour after hour and day after day, by those to whom Christ gives himself in Communion.

Among them, his life became the gift of the life of Christ, his life became the living word of Christ.

After going to seek out this handful of men at the edge of the world, he went to seek them out in the thickness of their lives; he shared in their conditions and slowly transformed and elevated them.

Then a day came when Jesus gave to the one who had so patiently given his life to him the gift of his death. "To constantly prepare oneself for martyrdom, to receive it without a shadow of defense", he had said.

He was betrayed by one of his own and murdered.

He received death without a word.

From all of this arose the other great lesson that Father de Foucauld gave and gives to our time.

The Gospel is not a book of historical studies: it is the face of Christ for us to imitate, his commandments for us to take literally and put into action.

He gave us the invaluable lesson that the words of Christ were not made to be recited or commented on, but to be taken literally, to be received by us as they were given to us by him.

He taught us that the only valid commentary on the Sermon on the Mount is our life, our lives in which those words fall like so many claps of thunder to shake us up and transform us.

He taught us that when Jesus says, "You are all brothers", it does not mean "You are theoretical members of the same theoretical family"; it means: "Do for every person you meet in life what you would do if he were your brother in the flesh."

That when Jesus tells us, "Blessed are the Poor", he is not necessarily speaking of others but of us, too.

That when Jesus says that "whoever exalts himself will be humbled", this does not mean that one can be a Christian and believe in the privilege of his social rank.

He taught us to listen to the Gospel as children who hear and obey.

He taught us that the preaching of the Gospel belongs to the priest in accordance with the words "but that one must proclaim the Gospel from the rooftops, through the whole of one's life."

He made us understand that if the Church seems to stay within the same confines, that if the Christian contagion does not spread as in the early days, it is perhaps because our life, the life of every Christian, is not the Gospel made flesh and blood where God has placed us.

He taught us that in love of God, everything is one, when we have consented to live in a permanent encounter with God.

That prayer generates the desire to imitate, that it requires the spirit of poverty and a disdain for what is grand. But that the one who configures himself to Christ becomes one with him, so that he cannot but love others in a practical way so long as he prays, and so long as he loves others, the most lost, the most sinful, the most in darkness attract him like a magnet attracts a pin.

He reminded us that the law of the Kingdom of Heaven is that, ever since the Cross, every victory begins with a failure, every mission by the burying of a seed, every life with death.

He reminds us that the love of Christ is not a comfortable and reassuring privilege but a splendid adventure that, visible or hidden, can never be lived without heroism.

Father de Foucauld always wanted brothers: he remained alone. But, since his death, a large spiritual family has been given to him. Direct, official relatives: unofficial and unknown relatives.

The Little Brothers, the Little Sisters, Le Tubet, Montpellier, the Fraternity, Father Monchanin, Father Henry, Charles Bouhier, Mission de Paris (priests and laity), Mission de France Féminine, Marseille.

Some as individuals in the world, others in teams.

Shared characteristics: God present, who jostles everything, taking the Gospel literally, the little ones, the most lost, complete charity, the absence of organized charity, evangelization: of God among men, work.

Far away

On the spot

Discovery of in-situ departures, of the journeys to be made in search of those civilized lands closed off to the Church.

Some departures that require leaving behind everything belonging to prior life with its traditions, its ways of thinking, its riches, in order to end up here where there are people and where the Kingdom of God has not yet come.

Liturgy and Lay Life (1947)

In 1947, in an issue from the series *Cahiers de la vie spirituelle* (Notebooks on the spiritual life), Madeleine published an article entitled "Liturgy and Lay Life". It is possible that this article was requested of her, even though, after the war, she sometimes wrote texts and sent them to reviews as a way of earning a bit of money for her group La Charité, always looking for contributions to give to those who knocked on the door and who were in need.

The series is entirely dedicated to prayer. In it we find prestigious names such as Fathers Paul Philippe, Th. Camelot, A. Plé, J.-M. Perrin, and L.-M. Dewailly —all Dominicans—or Father Paul-Marie of the Cross, a Carmelite, or Father René Voillaume, founder of the Little Brothers of Jesus (whose name appears only in the form of its initials). Three women contributed to the notebook: a member of the Young Christian Workers who remains anonymous and who speaks about her prayer life, Mademoiselle Melot, who wrote her article together with Father P.-M. Sirot, and Madeleine Delbrêl.

Madeleine's article was preceded by a long introduction written by the director of the review, A.-M. Henry, the text of which only paraphrases the article.

Madeleine contemplates the Church's two main forms

of prayer: the Office and the Mass. We might be surprised that she talks about the recitation of the Office by lay people. She does so from the perspective of a private devotion. Around 1931 or 1932, when they began to plan the way of life and spiritual rule for La Charité, Madeleine thought for a moment about the common prayer of the Office. Abbot Lorenzo held that the group was not a religious community. But Madeleine had "felt the hunger for this prayer of the Church", according to an expression that she used in her article. She also envisioned the prayer of the Office as a way for herself to pray in communion with the Church. Even though lay people are not under obligation to pray the Office, they can adapt it to their life, depending on the time they have and the circumstances that arise.

There was no breviary in French before the Council. However, adaptations began to be produced, such as the breviary of the Little Brothers of de Foucauld.

Regarding the Eucharist (Madeleine refers to the Mass according to the custom of the time), she participated in it daily and lived it as the source of her Christian existence at the same time as the privileged site of her communion with the ecclesiastical community. Thus it is always within the perspective of the Church that Madeleine discusses liturgical prayer, even when it is presented under the form of private prayer, as in the case of the Office. Which does not keep her from showing the ties that personal prayer maintains with the prayer of the Church, where it finds its source.

In this sense, especially concerning the prayer of the Office, she remarkably anticipates what has become, since the Second Vatican Council, a common property of the Christian community.

Two manuscript versions preceded the 1947 publication. The first, "Liturgy and Ordinary Life", had been extensively revised to constitute the second, "Liturgy and Lay Life". The version that follows is nearly identical to the published article.

~

When love of the Church has bitten our heart, her own prayer becomes almost necessary to us. Our soul prowls around the liturgy but often moves away discouraged.

This discouragement generally has two causes: either our daily life seems incompatible with an authentic liturgical life or our normal liturgical center, our parish, does not give us the prayer of the Church in a form that suits us.

So many of us moan about the famous "gap" that separates the parish prayer from the human masses; so many others suffer from adaptations that seem audacious to them; yet others, technicians of plain chant and of sacred art, are constantly stung by the exterior mediocrity of the rites; lastly, many others painfully feel all that money introduces into our churches on the occasions of marriages and deaths.

Therefore, perhaps it is not useless to pause over these obstacles before beginning our walk through the liturgy of ordinary people.

It is indispensable, facing this question, to have a dual attitude of soul.

First, to know that these obstacles, for us Christians, should remain small obstacles. In all that the Church gives us, there is the Spirit, and what are our little preferences, our poor little tastes, our poor little critiques compared to this contact with the Spirit of God?

To know also that if, for some pagans, certain superficial maladjustments might be detrimental, we must work to diminish them in a spirit and in an attitude of perfect charity. To injure charity even a little is to hurt the Church much more than the commercial aspect of some rites do.

And even when we think about the pagans while participating in certain parish functions, we must be careful not to sink into criticism or pessimism.

For the sake of these pagans, we would like for everything that the Church manifests to be outwardly impeccable and accessible.

Perhaps that is why it would be good for us to believe that the Church is a continuation of Jesus Christ and that if Jesus Christ wanted to be not the triumphal Messiah awaited by the Jews but the man of misconceptions, misunderstandings, and derision, no doubt it will always be permitted for something to remain misunderstood, unrecognized, and mocked in the Church.

In a service that we find to be outwardly perfect, we will have the joy of *seeing* people affected, moved.

In another service where we suffer—and suffer "as Church"—something distant and indecipherable, or worse, something worldly and profane, people will surely be affected on the *inside*, because we will have participated in the humiliations of Christ. And, in such a case, it is better to sink oneself, so to speak, in him, to make common cause with him, than to risk finding ourselves among the soldiers who mocked him.

For that matter, in the face of this group of relationships with God that constitutes the liturgy, under the pretext of human concern, let us not cease to be human, as we have been throughout the centuries. Every time men have wanted to give worship to God, they sought to clothe him in forms that approach the divine. They did not seek to understand everything, to reduce everything to their small size.

The liturgy is a thing of man and a thing of God. Let us love the two faces of it—its temporal face: the fresh flowers around the altar, the fresh wax that melts, the efforts of so many priests to bring it closer to us. But let us also love its eternal face: its language apart from the people's, its clothing outside time, its music beyond trends . . .

When it comes to these small material difficulties that make us consider the prayer of the Church practically inaccessible, let us trust the Holy Spirit, which is one of the paths, so that they do not manage to separate us from this great supernatural breath. By means that will not be either those of priests or those of nuns, we can participate in this prayer that itself inspires.

The notes that follow do not claim to be a systematic treatise. They are only reflections, born over the course of days, on encounters between the liturgy and life.

Concerning the Mass

The Mass for people who do not go.

There are those who can "assist" at Mass and those who cannot.

Let us begin with the latter, who are, again, of two sorts: either they are caught up in their work—that is the case for most mothers, and for those who are "hired" almost on the spot and begin early. Or there are those who, at Mass time, are on the bus or on the subway, unless illness keeps them in bed.

But whether we are there or not there: the Mass[1] is celebrated; whether we think about it or not, it is our Mass because we are Christians.

It is always a great benefit in not parting company with it.

---

[1] In the manuscript, Madeleine Delbrêl increased the use of capitalization for "Mass", "Saints", "Benediction", etc. . . . These capitalizations were removed from the text printed in the "Notebooks on the Spiritual Life".

If we cannot be present in a specific church, we retain the freedom to transport ourselves in spirit wherever our soul likes to go: the Mass of the Holy Father—Saint Peter's, holy places, the Mass of a priest friend, or simply that of our parish.

If we lose both Communion and everything that our material presence brings us, we win the easier discernment of that which, in a Mass, should last the whole day, both as an offering and as an intercession and as communion.

The Mass establishes us on a summit that is like the essence of our Christian life. From this summit, we must fall as little as possible.

The Mass, whether read in our bed or on the corner of a bench, puts us back in the presence of the core of our life, without which we have nothing to ease the current of our day.

But if this reading itself is not possible, to live one's Mass is always possible.

Those prayers which our memory has recorded take on a singular value when we blend them into the simple actions of our life.

They are so essentially Christian that our thought can attach itself to them without any division of the mind.

What action of our daily life can we approach for which the "Introibo ad altare Dei . . ."[2] is not appropriate?

---

[2] "I will approach the altar of God . . ."

What action of daily life does not leave an easy place for the cry of our heart: "Kyrie eleison"?

What vision of our days does not help us to bounce back in the "Gloria in excelsis"?

What work does not bring us together with a brother among our brothers to offer them all together with ourselves to the Father?

And so on until the benediction, which sends us into the world carrying the good news of the Word made flesh . . .

Conveyance to the Mass

But there are also those who can physically assist at Mass, every day or a few days a week.

I think that the Mass does not always yield all its fruit to us because we have not achieved the equivalent, in our life, of the kind of preparation for it that was present in religious life, or even the life of our grandparents, when the cities were not as big and more people were living in villages.

If the religious have, in the morning, a kind of conveyance of prayer that leads them to their Mass, this is neither superstition nor nonsense. It is knowledge of man. Nothing on earth is improvised. Fruits ripen . . . and so does our prayer.

Falling out of bed and into church, after running out of breath, leads us poorly to God.

Ten minutes more or less of sleep is not much. Ten minutes more between our rising and Mass is a lot.

This can prevent us from rushing. The small physical acts we have to do would already serve as a pre-Mass [preparation]. The trip to the church could be spent praying. *Losing* five minutes by acting slowly often *gains* us all the time we spend performing the action.

Likewise, when Mass is finished, it will often be an economy to shorten thanksgiving by a few minutes in order to return home peacefully or take our mode of transportation without haste.

In this resumption of contact with the world, let us remember the lesson of the Prophet Elijah, who, having sought God in the wind, the storm, and the thunder found him only in a very small breeze.

At the end of Mass, let us learn to leave room for a little breeze around our actions.

This place is free from all activity; it is never agitated.

Prayers

Every day, God presents a desire to our heart.

It is an act of obedience to surrender our heart to this desire.

It is expressed in the prayer of our Mass, and this prayer will return at every canonical hour in the Office.

Through this prayer, on the same day, are oriented the souls of all those who want to be, consciously, the Church. We all desire, through her, the same thing at the same time as the pope, the bishops, the religious, the Carthusians and the Carmelites, the missionaries of all the parts of the world.

Through this prayer, we can safely ask something for ourselves and for our brothers that we are sure is good, because it is God who wants to give it to us today.

Through this prayer, our heart feels useful. God makes use of it. Because if in the Psalms or the hymns, we often feel incorporated into the plan of the Spirit of God, and if we are invited to press our lips to the Word of God—in prayers, by contrast, it is God who comes to seek the desires, the feelings of our heart and make them his.

Because these prayers constantly request that we be strengthened, or pardoned, or enlightened, or calmed, or snatched away from evil, or repulsed by it.

Day by day, multitudes of souls throughout the world are providentially prepared to receive the fruit of this little prayer that the whole Church makes together. In reciting it, we are the "faithful and wise servant . . . to give them their food at the proper time". It is a ration of grace that we distribute to those who await it.

The prayer of the moment often occurs in the background.

Its seasonal character is reminiscent of farming tools: the plow, the combine, the sheaf-binder . . . It speaks of plowing and harvests.

Let us not forget to search for these good tools that are hidden in the corner of our missal and allow us to work for the bread of all.

The "Common"

When, in the note about the "saint of the day", a simple, short line puts us back in communion with martyrs, confessors, or virgins, we are a tiny bit disappointed. Our old individualism often enjoys cultivating that of others. The monotony surrounding the people of Heaven displeases us.

Through the "common" as through so many other things, the Church presents herself as educator. She who does not hesitate to endow a little nothing of a saint with a custom-made Office all the more does not hesitate to give to some of her most dazzling saints the "common" from "a to z". And perhaps this teaches us that all personal sanctity, all vocations of the soul, all incommunicable nuances cannot definitively situate themselves between these two poles, one of which is enormous and the other is infinite: the enormous original sin to which one must die, the immense love of the Father to which one must be born. Between these two are, of course, exquisite differences . . . but very small ones.

Statuit . . . In virtute tua . . . Os justi . . . Dilexisti[3] . . .

All the grand Offices that suit so well the multitude of those whose triumph they celebrate . . . those whose human exteriors were so different.

[3] From the first Latin words of the Mass shared by multiple saints.

The Office for Those Who
Do Not Have the Time

In the Office, it is our human time that prays.

The Church has covered time with a robe made out of the word of God.

Often, it is precisely our time that is lacking for this magnificent robe made to cover it.

We no longer have our time to ourselves. If some can harmoniously apportion their "hours" throughout the course of their days, they remain a tiny minority.

Yet, the reason for our conflict with the Office, for our "grinding" with it, comes from the fact that we want to engage in it like people who have time.

Almost always, when we have felt the hunger for this "prayer of the Church", we have resolved to recite this or that hour regularly—Lauds or Prime, Vespers or Compline. Life happens: it jostles, modifies, overloads, and it is in the middle of the day when we find ourselves facing Prime or in the middle of the night facing Compline.

Or again, for the sake of fidelity, having a quick quarter of an hour, we begin the recitation of our usual "hour". A rubric takes a little longer to find, we feel rushed, we are tense, maybe we are being ascetic, but our prayer becomes real work.

But while the slightly disciplinary and laborious side of the Office might be excellent for the religious whose long hours are spent in the choir, it is undoubtedly much less desirable and beneficial for people whose daily life already sets a record for overwork and tension.

For them, prayer, because it is relatively short, should be established in a maximum of peace.

For religious, the [time spent praying] Office in the choir will be doubled by the times of prayer, or rosary, or study, or quiet work.

For us, this prayerful break will often be inserted in the midst of much noise and agitation. Its mission will even be the calming of this agitation and noise.

If the Office does not retain a restful and expansive character for us, it will act contrary to its purpose, and instead of leading us to God by way of the Church, it will lead us to ourselves by way of our nerves and our exhausted attention.

I think that for many people caught up in a hectic daily life that is likely to remain hectic, there is a great blessing in not making too many "resolutions" with regard to the Office, other than remaining in *contact* with it.

We are free for a quarter of an hour? It is nine in the morning? Let us take up Prime.

We have a long trip at three: let us take up Vespers.

Let us take up Prime, let us take up Vespers, let us take up Compline . . . but let us never be sure of finishing them.

Let us walk gently in them, "beautifully", as Monsieur de Genève[4] would have said, hand in hand with the whole Church, heart to heart with Christ, heart to heart with the world. If our soul finds in such a verse a well of living water: let us give it time to drink it . . . and if we cannot finish, let us send an affectionate thought to those who, according to their state in life, will finish it.

Let us not think, either, that it is a waste of time, if our life is arranged in such a way that Compline or Prime fit in well, to spend several days studying its composition.

In a section about the recitation of the breviary, *La Vie spirituelle* (The spiritual life)[5] provided an analysis of Compline full of vigor and real life. Studies like this can reinvigorate our recitation of this or that hour.

It is also very useful to return often, in praying them, to the little phrases that return the most often in the Office. They are like the pivot. Automatism toward them will seriously truncate our prayer: the "*Domine exaudi*"[6] . . . the "*Amen*" . . . the "*Gloria*".

Just like those marine plants that, dried out, come alive again as soon as we put them in water, our Office will not be authentic unless we endlessly soak it in an ardent spirit of prayer. Without that, there will be a divorce between the letter and the spirit.

[4] Saint Francis de Sales, who was bishop of Geneva and a resident of Annecy France.

[5] *La Via spirituelle*, March 1946.

[6] "Lord, grant . . ."

Five Minutes in the Evening

Five minutes in the evening, and sometimes a little more, is, I believe, the indispensable condition for a good liturgical day.

Shuffling pages before Mass does not foster the soul's attention any more than racing to church does.

Preparing well for Mass is precious for those who can attend Mass: it is important, but it is even more important for those who can only live it.

Because the texts for Mass read in the evening are going to move in us, so to speak, during the night, and in the morning, we will feel them very close.

This prayer that will be the nagging desire for the new day: it is good for our heart to take on the form of it in advance, for us to whet our appetite from the evening onward for the graces we will have to request.

Lastly, it can be valuable for some of us who do very manual and monotonous work, to gather from tomorrow's Office some points of reference that, at every turn of the day, will be like tangible encounters with the Church: a phrase from a hymn, an antiphon, a verse . . .

In many cases, five minutes in the evening are, on level of the soul, akin to the moment when, also in the evening, we gather a meal to take with us the next day and put it in the lunchbox: "Man cannot live on bread alone . . ." He needs a little of the word of God.

Liturgy and Fatigue

In current times, fatigue of the nerves and fatigue of the brain are frequent.

"I cannot pray" is a phrase that often returns to the lips of the overworked, the depressed.

The portion of reflection that can occur in personal prayer is impossible for them. They succumb to a tumult of distractions or an invincible drowsiness, in any case, in a psychological climate that is bad for them. Reading is their refuge. But while it orients them toward God, it does not weld them to him like a real prayer.

The liturgy, well understood, could be restorative and calming for them.

Considering what we said above on the subject of tension and automatism, by intervening, if needed, with vocal prayer, we can lead weary spirits to a current of authentic and beneficial prayer.

The reading of the Gospel of the Mass can serve as a center for some scriptural study for them. The homily from Matins will be a whole that benefits from unity in variety.

Liturgical prayer is certainly one of those that carries the least risk of "splitting" us psychologically, and that is certainly why it is both invigorating and relaxing.

Prayer of Our Gestures

The Church does not forget that we have a body. In the gestures that she gives our body to do, let us not forget that we have a soul.

For this soul, in every liturgical gesture, hides a little grace: we will find it according to our hope.

Everything that is of the Church is trembling with life. It is we who have the sad ability to stupefy it by not allowing ourselves to wash in all these small gushing streams. It is the blood of Christ that wells up everywhere. Let us not grimace at the vessel that contains it: we have better things to do.

All these sublime or artless gestures are made in order for us to use them. A tiny act of faith before them might overturn more mountains than a liturgical revolution less laden with theological hope.

Toward "Communion" through Solitude[7]

Our modern life, even when it plunges us into the density of its crowds, often immerses us, at the same time, in a profound Christian solitude. The liturgy, with which we try to punctuate our days in the form of spiritual hinges, is almost always a liturgy of loners.

But let us be prudent! Under the pretext of finding the communion of saints through some morsel of the Office, let us not forget this small, visible "communion" of our parish, of our Catholic action movement, of our family.

Communal prayer is one of the great signs of the presence of Christ. There is no individual prayer that allows us to look down on it. The indication of our fidelity, of our liturgical sincerity, should be our joy in discovering parish Office, the community Mass of a movement, evening prayer, together, at home.

Every time God asks us to love the world, he suggests it to us through a minor encounter. The proof of a universal liturgical spirit is our willingness to live a few liturgical fragments sincerely with our brothers.

Obedience of the Soul

For we who remain "in this age" and must fully obey, let us be grateful to the liturgy for inclining our soul, the depth of our soul, toward the will of God.

Saint John of the Cross spoke of the "ecstasy of obedience". Liturgical ecstasy is constantly offered to us. Through it, we can pass immediately from our poor desires, from our myopic visions, to God's horizons.

Through it we can serve God, allow him to use us to ask him what pleases him.

Through it the "I" becomes "we". We lose ourselves without being subsumed in the multitude of God's singers, in the crowds of intercession.

Through it, every morning, we can surrender our soul to the impetus of the Holy Spirit living and pulsating in his Church.

Through it we babble the language of the children of God.

He Who Follows Me
Will Not Walk in Darkness (1948)

Little is known about the year 1948 in Madeleine's life. About the teams' lives, we mainly know that Raymonde Kanel left for three months, from January to March, to be a doctor in the Sahara with the Little Sisters of Jesus and that, at the end of the year, a new team was established in the industrial basin of Longwy. There were then four locations in four different regions: Ivry near Paris, Vernon in Eure, Cerisiers in Yonne, and Herserange near Longwy in Meurthe-et-Moselle.

From the year 1948, we have only five letters of Madeleine Delbrêl, short but full of meaning.[1] However, the period from 1945–1950 was a prolific one for writing, whether or not her creations can be precisely dated. During those postwar years, she wrote the meditations that have been collected in *Humour dans l'amour* (Humor in love).[2] She also wrote, gradually and in small books, of the adventures of an imaginary

---

[1] *S'unir au Christ en plein monde* (Paris: Nouvelle Cité, 2004), 163–67.

[2] *Œuvres complètes*, vol. 3, *Humour dans l'amour* (Paris: Nouvelle Cité, 2005).

person, Alcide,[3] about whom she offers short illustrated narratives to her friends and teammates. Apart from "The Dance of Obedience"[4] in 1949, none of these meditations were published in her lifetime.

And there is that text, a great meditation on the place the Gospel holds in the Christian life: "The Gospel is not a book among books. . . ." After the preceding texts about the Eucharist, Madeleine Delbrêl developed her thoughts on the Incarnation: "The Gospel . . . is the words of the Word of God; it is the Word of God made into a contemplated and recounted human life." And the "heart of flesh burns everything that it touches". We find here the themes of solitude, silence, and obedience initiated ten years earlier in "*We, the Ordinary People of the Streets*".

The archives have two typed manuscripts of *"Celui qui me suit . . ."* (He who follows me . . .) with different typewriting and nearly identical texts. The biblical references were established by the publishing team.

～

[3] *Œuvres complètes*, vol. 4, *Le Moine et le nagneau* (Paris: Nouvelle Cité, 2006), 25–92.

[4] *Humour dans l'amour*, 27. This meditation was published by Madeleine Delbrêl in *La Vie spirituelle* in August/September, 1949.

I

He who follows me will not walk in darkness.[5]

It is necessary to be aware of the two great dark masses between which our life is placed—the unfathomable darkness of God and the darkness of man—in order to surrender oneself madly to the Gospel, to discover it as the only decipherable path capable of making us live through the double nothingness of our state as creatures and our state as sinners.[6]

It is necessary to have plunged into the ambient death of that which makes our love human: devastations of time, of universal fragility, of sufferings; decomposition of all values, of human groups, of ourselves.

It is necessary, at the other pole, to have felt the universe impenetrable to the security of God in order to perceive in ourselves such a horror of darkness that the evangelic light becomes more necessary to us than bread.

Only then do we hold tightly to it as to a rope stretched above a double abyss.

It is necessary to know that one is lost in order to want to be saved.

[5] Jn 8:12.
[6] This first paragraph was poorly published in *Nous autres gens des rues* [We, the ordinary people of the streets] (Paris: Seuil, 1966), 79—paperback edition (Paris: Seuil, 1995), 72—to the point of changing the meaning.

The one who does not take in his hands the thin book of the Gospel with the resolution of a man who has only one hope can neither decipher it nor receive the message from it.

No matter, then, that this hopeless blessed one, lacking all human expectation, takes this book from the shelf of a rich library, or from his heavy jacket pocket, or from a student's satchel; no matter if he grabs it during a break in his life or on a day like any other; in a church or in his kitchen, in the countryside or in his office—he will grab the book, but he himself will be grabbed by the words that are spirit. They will penetrate him like the seed in the earth, like the leavening in the dough, like the tree in the air, and he, if he consents, will be able to become simply a new expression of these words.

Herein is the great mystery hidden in the book of the Gospel.

Every book is already a mystery: a mystery of man. In every book there is a junction of matter and spirit, of signified and invisible. Every book demonstrates that the frontiers of the soul are beyond the flesh and that its dimensions cannot be touched with the hands.

But the Gospel is not just a book among books. It is not a word of man among the words of men; it is the word of the Word of God, it is the Word of God made into contemplated and recounted human life.

In it is an illuminating and transformative virtue, a permanent and powerful gift from God.

But every gift from God is poured only into the

hands of faith; every gift from God is received only in the vertiginous depths of hope.

In order to deliver its mystery, the Gospel does not require a setting, or erudition, or a technique; it requires a soul prostrated in adoration and a heart stripped of all man's confidence.

II

He who does what is true comes to the light.[7]

I have given you an example, that you also should do as I have done to you.[8]

He who has my commandments and keeps them, he it is who loves me.[9]

The secret of the Gospel is not a secret of curiosity, an intellectual initiation: the secret of the Gospel is essentially a communication of life.

The light of the Gospel is not an illumination that remains outside of us: it is a fire that demands to penetrate us in order to bring about a devastation and a transformation there.

He who allows a single word of the Lord to penetrate him and allows it to be realized in his life, knows more about the Gospel than the one whose entire ef-

[7] Jn 3:21.
[8] Jn 13:15.
[9] Jn 14:21.

fort is applied to abstract meditation or historical consideration.

The Gospel was not made for spirits in search of ideas.

It was made for disciples who want to obey.

The Obedience required of a disciple of Jesus Christ, kneeling before the word and example of his master, is not a discursive, reasoning, interpretative obedience; it is a child's obedience, returned to its radical ignorance as a creature, to its universal blindness as a sinner.

Facing these simple and ruthless instructions, there is no giving our "maybe" and our "more or less"; all that is possible is the "yes" that opens life to us and the "no" that closes us off in death. These words were made in order to reach the roots of corruption in us, whose depths we cannot fathom because we are ignorant of the high place where our sanctity resides. So we should not be surprised by the interminable and painful journeys, the inner turmoil that each of these words works in us. We must not stop this kind of descent of the word into our depths. We need the passive courage to let it act in us. "Let it be done unto me according to your word."

And when a single one of these words has stolen us away from ourselves, we will need to know how to desire to be in communion with everyone else, even if this little book seems immense to us and our life utterly minuscule, narrow, and incapable of supporting it.

III

My words are spirit and life.[10]

It is the spirit that gives life, the flesh is of no avail.[11]

The revelation of the Gospel is spirit and life . . . It demands as its audience the spirit and life of the one who wants to receive it. We often think about giving it the "letter" of our existence, of time, of material solitude, of escapes. When our mode of existence prevents us, we readily believe that the Gospel is not for us, or that there is only a mutilated or falsified Gospel for us.

We would willingly leave to those who have opted for the Desert the fullness of a message that was lived and preached in the most intimate depth of the world.

However, it is all our lives that are called to be "evangelized", that have the vocation to receive the whole word of Jesus Christ. But they cannot receive it unless they give themselves as themselves, as lives, as our lives. They cannot receive it unless they give themselves with all their internal energies, with all their lifeblood, with all their spirit.

It is in our life, which, from morning to evening, flows between the banks of our house, of our streets, of our encounters, that the word of God wants to reside.

[10] Jn 6:63.
[11] Jn 6:63.

It is in our spirit, which makes us who we are through the acts of our work, our sorrows, our joys, our loves, that the word of God wants to dwell.

The Lord's sentence that we have extracted from the Gospel at morning Mass or in a subway ride, or between two household chores, or in the evening in our bed, must no longer leave us, any more than our life or our spirit leaves us. It wants to fertilize, modify, renew the handshake that we have to give, our effort in our task, our gaze upon those we meet, our reaction to fatigue, our jolt of pain, our fulfillment in joy.

It wants to be at home everywhere that we are at home.

It wants to be us everywhere that we are ourselves.

The word of the Lord commands our respect.

If our life has possible breaks, [the word of the Lord] wants simultaneously to possess a little or a lot of these pauses; it demands that our spirit occupy itself exclusively with it, wants from it the sacrifice of all that is worth less than it. It wants us to pray over it, oblivious of everything that is so little compared to it.

If our life is so crowded with our duties that the breaks are impossible, if our children, a husband, the house, the work invades almost everything, the word of the Lord wants us to believe enough in it, to respect it enough, to know that its divine power will always make room for it. So we see it glow while we walk in the street, while do our work, while we peel our vegetables, while we wait for a phone call, while we sweep our floors. We see it glow between two of our neighbor's sentences and between two letters to write, when we wake up and when we go to sleep.

This is because it will have found its place, a heart of man, poor and warm, to receive it.

IV

I am ascending to my Father and to your Father, to my God and to your God.[12]

To receive the Gospel message in our life is to allow our life to become, in the broad and real sense of the word, a religious life, a life related, bound up with God.

The essential revelation of the Gospel is the dominant and invasive presence of God.

It is a call to encounter God, and God is only encountered in solitude.

To those who live among men, it seems this solitude is denied.

This would be to believe that we precede God in solitude: it is he who waits for us, to find him is to find it, because true solitude is spirit, and all our human solitudes are but relative steps toward the perfect solitude that is faith.

True solitude is not the absence of men; it is the presence of God.

To put one's life face to face with God, to surrender

[12] Jn 20:17.

one's life to the notion of God, is to leap into a realm where we are made solitary.

It is their height that creates the solitude of the mountains, and not the place where their bases are set.

If the bursting forth of God's presence in us rises in silence and solitude, it leaves us situated, blended, radically united with all the people who are made of the same earth as us.

To those who consent to this solitary encounter with God, God additionally gives the solitude of man. He makes us understand that, after subtracting [man's] gifts, his drives, his desires, all that remains is a kind of communal dough made from the same nothingness and the same sin, where man only sees in other men a sad and monotonous extension of himself.

In this unvarying mud, the only discernably distinctive things are the creative and redemptive wishes of God; they call forth our enthusiasms and our loves. Yes, we see them gushing forth from him; they do not distract us from him; they spread his solitude over the whole world.

V

Moments of Solitude

Like the one who left Paris for the Desert smiles at solitude from afar; like the voyager who waits with a heart expanded by the long days spent at sea; like the monk who caresses the walls of his cloister with his eyes, as soon as he wakes—let us open our soul to the little solitudes of the day.

Because our minuscule moments of solitude are as great, as exultant, as holy as all the deserts of the world, they are inhabited by the same God, the God who makes solitude holy.

Solitude of the dark street that separates the house from the subway, solitude of a bench where others carry their part of the world, solitude of the long hallways where flows the current of all the lives on the way toward a new day. Solitude of a few minutes where, crouching in front of the stove, we wait for the kindling to light before putting in the coal, solitude of the kitchen before the bowl of vegetables. Solitude on bended knee on the floor that we scrub, in the garden path where we go to fetch a bit of lettuce. Little moments of solitude on the stair climbed up and down a hundred times a day. Solitude of long hours of laundry, of mending, of ironing.

Moments of solitude we might dread and that are the hollowing out of our heart: loved ones who go and whom we want to stay; friends whom we wait for and who do not come; things we would like to say and no one listens, strangeness of our heart among men.

The first step in solitude is a departure. Real deserts are gained, in the two senses of the word, in taking the train, the boat, and the plane. We do not know how to discern the multiple little departures that punctuate a day; that is why we do not always succeed in our own moments of solitude, in the moments of solitude that have been prepared for us.

Because an interlude of solitude is separated from us by only the thickness of a door or by the span of a quarter hour, we deny it its value of eternity, we do not take it seriously, we do not approach it as a unique landscape, capable of essential revelations.

It is because our heart lacks expectation that the wells of solitude scattered throughout our days deny us the living water with which they overflow.

We have the superstition of time.

If "our love takes time", God's love makes light of the hours, and a receptive soul can be overwhelmed by him in an instant.

"I will allure her, and bring her to the wilderness, and speak tenderly to her."[13]

If our moments of solitude are poor abductors of the Word for us, it is because our heart is absent from them.

VI

Blessed are those who hear the word of God and keep it![14]

There is no solitude in silence.

Sometimes silence means keeping quiet, but silence always means listening.

An absence of noise that is empty of our attention to the word of God would not be silence.

A day full of noise and full of voices might be a day of silence if the noise becomes the echo of the

[13] Hos 2:14.
[14] Lk 11:28.

presence of God for us, if the voices are messages and solicitations from God for us.

When we speak of ourselves and through ourselves, we come out of silence.

When we repeat, with our lips, the private suggestions of the word of God deep within us, we leave silence intact.

Silence does not like the profusion of words.

We know how to speak or how to be quiet, but we do not know how to be content with [only] the words that are necessary. We constantly oscillate between a muteness that damages charity and an explosion of words that overruns the truth.

Silence is charity and truth.

It responds to the one who asks something of it, but it only gives words charged with life. Silence, like all guidelines in life, leads us to the gift of ourselves and not to a disguised avarice. But it keeps us gathered for this gift. We cannot give ourselves when we have been dispersed. The vain words that inhabit our thoughts are a constant squandering of ourselves.

"For all your words, we will be held accountable."[15]

For all those [words] that needed to be said and that our greed held back.

For all those [words] that needed to be held back and that our prodigality scattered to the four winds of our fancy or of our nerves.

---

[15] Cf. Lk 11:50–51.

VII

Silences

How can the wind in the pines, the storm on the sand, the gusts over the sea count as silence, but not the pounding of machines in the workshop, the rumbling of trains in the station, the hubbub of cars in the intersection?

Here, as there, these are the great laws of God at play, rustling the creation that surrounds us.

Why do the singing of a skylark in the wheat, the chirping of insects in the night, the buzzing of bees in the thyme nourish our silence, and not the footsteps of crowds in the street, the voices of women at the market, the cries of men at work, the laughter of children in the garden, the songs that drift out of bars? Everything is the noise of creatures that are advancing toward their destiny, everything is the echo of God's house, in order or in disorder, everything is a sign of life encountering our life.

Silence is not an escape, but the gathering of ourselves in the hollow of God.

Silence is not a snake in the grass that the slightest noise makes flee; it is an eagle of strong wings who overlooks the hubbub of the earth, of men, and of wind.

VIII

Pray then like this: Our Father who art in heaven . . .[16]

He who "prays" "Our Father who art in heaven" and who lives as a child of the earth is a liar.

In order to stop being a liar, he must convert.

Our roots are in the earth.

We have to put them in heaven.

In order for the tree of our life to push its branches on the earth so that the birds can nest there, it must be planted upside down.

The cross on which Saint Peter was crucified upside down is the image of the whole evangelic life.

The life that we receive from the earth ages us at every moment.

The life that we seek close to the Father establishes us in a youth that is renewed at every moment.

The strengths we demand from earthly nourishments, the energies that we solicit from all human medicines, replenish our weakness, but leave it incurably weak.

When our weakness cries out to God, it becomes the place of the strong God.

The lights that we beg from everything that illuminates the world leave our eyes myopic and their visual field narrow.

[16] Mt 6:9.

When we close them under God's touch, it is they themselves that are changed and learn to see, even in the dark.

The love we try to live by throwing ourselves into the lives of others leaves our heart inconceivably variable: sometimes ardent and sometimes cold, sometimes tender and sometimes like stone.

When we turn our heart toward God, he gives us "this heart of flesh" that also burns everything it touches.

In truth, to pray "Our Father" is to renounce the progression of death in us in order to let ourselves be born to eternal life.

M. D. 1948

The People of Paris Go to
Their Father's Funeral (1949)

Cardinal Emmanuel Suhard, archbishop of Paris since 1940, died on May 30, 1949. He was very involved in efforts for the missionary revival of the Church of Paris and of France. His pastoral letter for Lent 1947 has remained famous: "The Rise or Fall of the Church". Here are a few words from it: "Far from leading to the conclusion of its decline, everything foreshadows its rise! We will only say—and these will be our instructions for action—what are, for the present, the conditions of this Springtime."[1]

He announced a springtime for the Church, a springtime that required renewed commitment. Madeleine Delbrêl was in personal contact with the cardinal. Christine de Boismarmin attested: "When an important question arises, whether about the small group for which she is responsible, or for herself, she asks to see him. It is one of his strong opinions that she is ahead of her time."[2] He wrote to her personally with these words in January 1949: "I rely heavily on your vo-

[1] *Essor ou déclin de l'Église*, Lettre Pastorale, Carême de l'an de grâce 1947, les éditions du Vitrail, 11 (The rise or fall of the Church: A pastoral letter from Lent in the year of grace 1947).

[2] Cf. Christine de Boismarmin, *Madeleine Delbrêl, rues des villes Chemins de Dieu (1904–1964)* (1985), 98; (ed. 2004), 130.

cation . . ."[3] It was a father who died, an archbishop close to the living strength of the Church.

~

When the father dies, the children go to the funeral: they are the first behind the coffin.

The people of Paris had lost their Father. They went to Notre Dame—the people who believed and also the people who did not believe.

They came with their prayers, or with their sympathy, or with their respect, or with their curiosity.

They arrived at the church, and the church was closed. At 8 o'clock it was closed, at 9 o'clock it was still closed, at 10 o'clock it was still closed.

They thought that people were not allowed to enter before the Father entered, so that all his children would follow him and enter with him. But the church was open for the priests and religious, for official personages, for those who had invitations.

The people of Paris thought that this was perhaps more practical, and they waited their turn, their place, with the family, behind the body.

The square was full of people, full of folded hands, of inquiring looks.

They buzzed with questions.

The loudspeakers were barely working: it was a shame.

[3] Ibid., (ed. 1985), p. 98; (ed. 2004) p. 131.

When the procession had entered, the people of Paris wanted to follow it, but the barricades did not yield.

By chance or kindness, a handful of people were able to pass through, were able to enter. I was one of them. The others remained outside.

Even if the church had been full, it would have been difficult to leave the people of Paris at the door.

But the church was not full.

Notre Dame is made to receive the people of Paris. She is used to it.

If the people were outside, it is because Notre Dame was not full.

There were many empty seats in the back of the side aisles. The side chapels were empty. Empty, too, the huge galleries on each side of the nave.

When the ceremony was over, the people of Paris wanted to come close to their Father.

But they were not yet wanted.

We asked them to wait an hour and a half in front of a deserted church. Their time was precious, and it was raining.

Those who believed had raised their hearts toward the Father who had known how to understand them, and their heart was heavy with a double pain.

Those who did not believe no doubt believed even a little less.

They could not encounter, through this cold and organized pomp, the divine and maternal tenderness that might have waited for them behind the stones.

Mission and Missions (1950)

Father Jacques Loew,[1] who converted as a young adult
like Madeleine Delbrêl and who became a Dominican
and one of the first worker-priests of France, a docker
in Marseille as well as the pastor of the parish of la
Cabucelle, wrote a long and passionate introduction
to the collection *Nous autres gens des rues* (We, the ordinary people of the streets),[2] published in 1966, two
years after Madeleine Delbrêl's death.

He quotes a long excerpt from the personal notes
that follow, emphasizing these words with their Pauline
accents: "The Christian is a captive."[3]

On four handwritten pages, and a fifth that contains
nothing but a title, Madeleine Delbrêl wrote treasures
that remain the sketches of an artist. Then she takes up
the idea again on larger canvases. But this outpouring
of writing has a strength that did not deceive someone like Jacques Loew. The whole text highlights the
"dimensions that on the whole are no longer ours".

---

[1] See the article by Bernard Pitaud, "Madeleine Delbrêl and
Jacques Loew", *Madeleine Delbrêl: Genèse d'une spiritualité*, 229–
314.

[2] *Nous autres gens des rues* (Paris: Seuil, 1966), 9–53; paperback
edition (Paris: Seuil, 1995), 9–50.

[3] Ibid. (ed. 1966), 21; paperback edition (Paris: Seuil, 1995),
20.

Despite its fragmentary nature, we have chosen to publish it.

~

To be a missionary is not to be a propagandist for this or that idea, even a Christian one.

It is not even a kind of specialization within the Christian life.

To be a missionary is no more *optional* than it is *exceptional*.

A Christian cannot afford not to be, in one way or another, a missionary.

Just as being a missionary does not authorize him not to be totally Christian.

The missionary state is part of the plenitude of the Christian life: some will understand this first, others last, it matters little: in fact, that is the way it is.

The missionary, because he is a Christian, is a captive.

The captive of a life: the life of Christ (not the propagandist of an idea, but the member of a body who lives and who wants to believe).

The captive of a thought: he is not a free thinker (not the propagandist of an idea, but the voice of another: "the voice of his Master").

The captive of a momentum: of a God-sized desire that wants to save what is lost, heal what is sick, unite what is separated, perpetually and universally.

To be a Christian is to be the captive of a state of affairs, the captive of dimensions that, on the whole, are no longer ours; the captive, if I may say so, of a freedom that has been chosen for us in advance.

It is in this captivity that the missionary must announce the Christ that he lives, announce a message that he has received and that he must not modify, transmit a salvation that does not come from him and that is the size of the whole world.

He is a captive of this Christ whom he lives and cannot modify.

He is a captive of this message that he cannot correct.

He is a captive of this salvation that he cannot restrain.

These points of view could lead to a whole survey of the tearing apart to which we have to submit because we are missionaries:

1. in the sole mission of Christ and because we are missionaries in this or that Mission of the Church: Mission of Marseille, of Paris, of such-and-such a corner of France,

2. and in the sectors of the world, which, paganized, call for a particular expression, like others, because they are missionaries in China, in Spain, or in Hungary.

I do not intend to make this survey because I do not intend for us to speak together for a few months or a few weeks.

I would just like to locate some of the crossroads where we are situated.

Poverty

We can be called to a *poverty*—we do not have the right to say that only this is evangelical poverty, any more than we have the right to ignore the evangelical poverty in our life.

At present, poverty appears in France as a pressing need of the Church.

Preach the Gospel to every creature

Proletariat and Little Ones
The "other"
The individual and the collective

Mysticism of the Work and work of the Kingdom

Church and Mission
(1950–1951)

Following the preceding text, which is a sketch, here is the finished text. The manuscript is written in a very clear and fully mature style. Madeleine Delbrêl, according to a very Pauline consciousness, describes the situation of a Christian, a captive of Christ and also free because Christ is supremely free. This engages him in a state of life, work, and thought that Madeleine develops in the three parts in her text: "State of Life", "Work of the Christ Church", "The Thought of Christ".

This text was published in 1966 in *Nous autres gens des rues* (We, the ordinary people of the streets). It is dated 1951. However, considering its successive link to a letter from July 10, 1950, that Madeleine Delbrêl addressed to Jacques Loew,[1] we are publishing it here, for in the second part, she resumes her letter to Jacques Loew. A few sentences are quoted as they are, but the whole text is reworked. On the other hand, a precise study of the manuscript leads us to believe that the 1966 editors themselves inserted two excerpts of this letter in their publication and, conversely, deleted

---

[1] *S'unir au Christ en plein monde* (Paris: Nouvelle Cité, 2004), p. 196.

a few sentences. Of course, we have restored them. The footnotes will guide the reader who would like to understand better what they are.

~

The purpose of the following notes is to elucidate the attitude of Christians—who are missionaries because they are Christians—who, if they feel the need for commitment in their lives, perceive, to the same extent, the need for detachment.

They do not demand that all vocations conform to theirs, but they try to situate the direction they feel compelled to take in the current Church-World situation.

Through his Baptism, the Christian exchanged his freedom for the freedom of Christ.

He is free because Christ is supremely free, but he no longer has the right to choose:

a *state of life* other than that of Christ

an *action* other than that of Christ

a *thought* other than that of Christ.

It is the state of living Faith.

Faith is an established fact for him, and he has only to accept it.

This *state of life* is to be a child of God in Christ with all his brothers who are Christ with him. Facing God and facing the world, in God and in the world, it is with *all* the others that he is Christ. He is completely Christ, the Christ Church: it is an established fact about which he can do nothing.

This *action* is not a small individual matter.

It is connected, welded, to the very action of God, to this "action that is endless", to this action that is holy history, the history of the Church, the history of the City of God. The missionary has *his* move to make, but this move is but a ripple in the *perpetual* and *universal* momentum of the Holy Spirit. It is surrounded on all sides by others that prepare it, complement it, continue it.

This *thought* is designed by the Truth that is Christ. What it brings to this design is comparable to the information that the sensory organs bring to the brain: they insert themselves as general data and are assessed and used by it.

This state of life, this action, this thought are for *Christ's great project*, the work of Christ, which is the salvation of the world.

The work of the Church is the salvation of the world.

The world can only be saved by the Church.

The Church is only the Church because she saves. We are not the Christ Church if we are not saviors.

We are not saviors if we are not the Church.

And we are not the Church if we are not the *whole* Church: every member belongs to the whole body.

And we are not the whole Church unless we are exactly in our place within her, which is equivalent to being exactly in the place in the world where it is present through us.

Church and Mission

The mission is to do the very work of Christ wherever we are.

We will not be the Church, we will not spread salvation to the ends of the world, unless we work for the salvation of the men among whom we live.

And we will not work for this salvation, we will not let it get through, unless we are inalterably, purely the Church in their midst.

We are in a world where salvation does not seem to get through. Another piece of the world "wrongly keeps most of the blood or food of this body for itself".

We must suffer this unto death.

But we must make sure that giving life to some does not mean preparing mortal agony tomorrow for others.

It is not Peter or John who must strive for the salvation of a small or large group of men; it must be the Church who, through Peter and John, finds this group of men, because it is only the Church who can truly find them.

The Mission-Church

1. State of Life

Therefore, the Mission must be the Church.

She must be the "body of Christ"; afterward, she is free to choose her paths.

She must accept her *total state of Christ.*

"That they may be one as we are one."[2]

"If you were of the world, the world would love its own; but because you are not of the world, but I chose you out of the world, therefore the world hates you."[3]

To please the world, to be loved by the world, even if this world is made of our nonbelieving brothers, cannot be weighed against unity among Christians.

We do not have to choose; our freedom is not our own. The arm does not choose to be connected to the tree from which it gathers fruit: it belongs to the body, even if the body is too far from the tree.

If we harm Christian unity in order to speak to unbelievers about Christ, we prefer to give an echo of what Christ is, to give Christ in his sacrament par excellence: Christians united among themselves.

It was required of Israel to be the People of God among peoples, and that everything should be sacrificed for the sake of this.

We are required to be, in the midst of the social human body, the visible body of Christ God: and for this, everything should be sacrificed.

If this unity has cohesion, it also has a vital meaning.

Obedience in the body of Christ is also an established fact.

The blood flows in one direction. It only reaches the

[2] Jn 17:11.
[3] Jn 15:18-19.

fingertips after going through many stages. We cannot change this direction.

Authority in the Church can crush us, cast shadows over us: we must obey because for us this is to live, and it would be insane for a living organism to prefer this or that action over life.

It is not up to us to change the places of organs in the body.

We cannot put our eyes on our fingertips nor our heart in our head. Similarly, a mystic or a missionary cannot replace the "hierarchy" for us. We fall into the trap of words, and this word "hierarchy" tends to become a concept for us.

Yet this word signifies the communication of Christ to every organ of his body.

It is Christ teaching, directing, clarifying, sanctifying.

This gift remains intact even in crippled, even corrupted, forms.

Israel, because it dreamed of a triumphant Messiah, did not recognize its God crowned with thorns and covered in spittle.

Because we dream of a Christ Church triumphant in the eyes of men, we do not always know how to remember that the mystery of Christ is the mystery of the Church and that, until the end of time, it will be the Savior humiliated, disguised in men, limited and sinful men, and that it is in them that we must recognize him.

The revaluation of our character as baptized and confirmed, the "adulthood of the laity", should not lead us to believe ourselves to be invested in all the "functions" of Christ.

Just because Baptism made us "Christ", it did not give us all the functions of Christ.

The most "adult" lay person is lower in a certain order of grace than the most "minor" priest because in the priest there is a communication with Christ in which the lay person does not participate.

This does not mean the lay person should be passive.

He has to "become what he is", which generally infinitely surpasses what he manages to be.

He has to demand constantly from his priests and his bishops what, in justice, he can expect from them, and the absence of which puts him in a state of supernatural misery.

But it is *they* who must ultimately give it to him.

No more than he can be "separate" from all the others in the Church, the Christian cannot be in just any place.

Here again it is not up to him to choose.

It is always Faith as a statement of fact.

2. Work of the Christ Church

The "work" of the Christ Church is that "the world be saved".

By the cross that makes children of God in Christ.

By the Gospel that teaches how to live as a child of God.

The cross is not optional either for the world or for us.

The cross accepted and the cross taken up are the main part of our work.

This work of the cross is itself also a statement of fact in us: "You are crucified with Christ."[4] It is our foundational work. The rest follows.

"If any man would come after me, let him deny himself and take up his cross", and only after, "and follow me."[5] It is in Christ crucified that the world is potentially saved, and it is a suffering world, and one that will remain suffering, to which we must give the Joy of Christ.

To save the world is not to give it happiness.

It is to give it the meaning of its pain and a joy "that no one can take away".

While we must fight against the woes and misfortunes that Christ took seriously so that on the last day we are judged according to the help we gave him, we must remember that, beyond them, it is about eternal life and not a second Earthly Paradise.[6]

---

[4] ". . . I have been crucified with Christ" (Gal 2:19).

[5] Mt 16:24, Mk 8:34, Lk 9:23.

[6] In the text *Nous autres gens des rues* (We, the ordinary people of the streets) (1966 edition), p. 121; paperback edition (Paris: Seuil, 1995), 111, there is a paragraph added here that does not exist in the manuscript. It is in fact an excerpt of a letter to Jacques Loew from July 10, 1950, cited unaltered from "Mais si le Royaume" to "identification à lui mais un don". Cf. *S'unir au Christ en plein monde,* pp. 203–4. A little farther in the publication of *Nous autres gens des rues,* p. 127, is a note that is also a quotation from the same letter to Jacques Loew. All this led us to believe that the 1966 editors knew of the connections between the letter

The Gospel is to be announced.

Here rise all the walls that prevent the Evangelists from being heard or getting through.

It is here that all the breaches must be made, all the bridges must be built.

Except that, in making these breaches, building these bridges, and letting our voices be heard, we do not declare ourselves satisfied.

It is not only a matter of passing through, not only a matter of speaking, of being heard and of "pleasing"— the message spoken by us must be intact.

At the crossroads where we stand, a certain number of points call for our attention.

The Gospel is the announcement made to men of the possibility of being made righteous in Christ. It is not the announcement of the establishment of a human justice.

Christ came to make us righteous. He did not come to deliver justice.

"The poor have good news preached to them."[7]

The Good News is brought to them.

It does not say that "poverty will be eliminated."

Quite the contrary: "You always have the poor with you."[8]

and

"Blessed are the poor."

---

of July 10, 1950, and "Church and Mission". They seemed to have wanted to fuse the two.

[7] Mt 11:5.

[8] Mt 26:11, Mk 14:7, Jn 12:8.

Because of this beatitude, the Christian tends toward poverty: Why would he tend to want, through love, to lift others out of it or make the suppression of this poverty the condition for salvation?

To evangelize the Poor is not to make them rich or to think that evangelization is conditioned on first enriching them.

This is contrary to the entire history of Christ in the world.

The Gospel has never been rejected because of poverty or hardship, from the slaves of Rome to the dockworkers of Corinth, up to the German [concentration] camps.

It is the wealth of those who are to announce the Gospel that can impede its spread. It is the Christians who are rich in any way whatsoever.

We have to make ourselves poor in order to announce the Gospel.

It is not a poor world that obstructs the expansion of the Gospel but the rich sectors of the Church.

Preach the Gospel:

The good news of the Kingdom of God and not that of a better world.

We must not forget the *"one direction"* of salvation that can only come from God through Christ.[9]

---

[9] From "the '*one* direction' of salvation" until "the perspective should be respected", this passage is a reprisal from the letter Madeleine Delbrêl sent to Jacques Loew on July 10, 1950. *S'unir au Christ en plein monde*, pp. 197–200. Madeleine Delbrêl reused certain whole sentences and rewrote others.

We must not blend the Gospel of salvation with the recipes for happiness that the world so cherishes.

We must not attribute to the world the authorship of certain popular ideas that are actually pieces of the Gospel separated from their context and taken over by human sectors.

We must not unite the message of Christ to other messages, making it an element of the salvation of man by man, putting the Gospel in the service of causes that are not purely and simply that of salvation. From one end to the other, the Gospel cries out to us that God alone is, that the world itself creates neither life, nor truth, nor love.

The Kingdom of Heaven is the personal love of God, in Christ, for *each* of us and of *each* of us for each other. It is through the love of *each* person that we can love humanity.

It is *each* individual who must receive the Gospel. Salvation is not a collective abstraction.

The world itself oscillates between two poles, where "each person" is sacrificed to an abstraction.

Because selfish capitalism practically rejects all the others in collective misery in the name of the well-being of a few, and because Marxism, in the name of a better-off collective, rejects "the dissenters" who are also living in poverty, we risk losing the unique meaning that the Evangelization and salvation have.

The Kingdom of God is the encounter of God and a humanity composed of 1+1+1.

It does not arise from an anonymous mass but is

received by Peter, James, John, and communicated by them to other Peters, Jameses, and Johns.

The Kingdom of God is the love, not of the world, but of men.

The world is not an absolute reality: it is relative, a possibility constantly being modified by the interplay of good and evil forces in all the hearts of all men.

The Gospel of the Kingdom tells us that the world is not important. It is men who are important because it is what they are. The world is the living ones of every day who make and unmake it. It is not in working for the world that we will make it better: it is every better man who makes a better world.

A world rebuilt by our hands, which works by a kind of acquired momentum and ultimately gives salvation, is an abstraction.

We do not have to seek to align the outcome of the "Kingdom of God" and the outcome of the world. It is not the sum of righteous cities that will constitute the heavenly Jerusalem, but the sum of all the love that, in a small or great Church, composed of many or few saints, extended to familiar and unfamiliar men, will revive Redemption for a multitude.

The Kingdom of God and the world do not necessarily align. Periods of chaos, of cruelty, can give rise to passions, to an intensity of faith generative of salvation. The progression of the Kingdom of God in the world is for the purpose of eternity: the means should interest us insofar as the end interests us; but the perspective should be respected.[10]

If the confusion of the two planes—the world and Kingdom of Heaven—has led the men who make up the Church into unholy alliances with capitalism, we must not, under the pretext of breaking away from that, risk welding [the Church] to other systems that, because they are temporal and of the world, would weigh it down tomorrow with chains similar to those from which we would like to free it today.

The "narrow" but positive way of the Gospel runs through a labyrinth of possible missteps.

"That they may all be one . . . so that the world may believe that you have sent me."[11]

Unity returns here with promises of redemptive efficacy.

To strive for unity among Christians is not to cease to be a missionary: it is to establish the very condition of evangelization.

The Truth Will Set You Free[12]

Alongside the "economic" liberations that the world preaches and which, upon closer examination, are only a kind of getting comfortable with the bonds of human needs, Christ proclaims the liberation from Evil.

[10] End of the reuse of passages from the aforementioned letter to Jacques Loew.
[11] Jn 17:21.
[12] Jn 8:32.

Yet, while many Christians accept this liberation from evil in their individual lives, most of them accept the dictatorship of evil in practice in its social manifestations.

Some of them cut their life in two and fit a sincere Christian life into a framework built by the world they think they cannot change: employers, formerly professional careers, business.

Others, considering all these social sectors as definitively "possessed" by the spirit of evil, flee in the name of poverty and love into the mass of the little ones and the poor.

This is the departure of many bourgeois or intellectual elements toward the proletariat.

If this step appears necessary for a new springtime of the Gospel, it appears also only as a step, and perhaps the easiest.

There is no class that is "damned from heaven" in the Gospel.

The social "status" of men seems of no interest to Christ.

In the Gospel, he commands humble people to leave their jobs.

To Lazarus, to the Centurion, to Nicodemus, he does not command that they go fishing: he asks them for something else: a renewal of heart, an essential conversion, which in each of their lives will make everything new.

Saint Paul does not himself attack slavery, but it is

the heart of Christians, evangelized by him, who will no longer support owning slaves.

If the renewal of heart of some leads them to share in the life of the worker, we must believe, I think, that this is but a small part of the question, that a multitude of hearts have to turn themselves around and *explode* where they are, cracking the mask of the world, so that where they are, the true face of Christ appears.

It seems, then, that in this vast horizon, we were singularly lacking in genius, in the spirit of invention . . . or, in short, the Spirit.

Those who have ventured near, with a few exceptions, have done so only with infinite timidity.

Here again we find the recipe for a temptation opposite to the Spirit's demands.

The mystical "duty of one's state in life" risks accepting the unacceptable.

The mystical "structure" on which we immediately wish to connect, not Peter or James, but this or that bourgeois or economic milieu, shortens and binds the supremely free and renewing initiatives of the Spirit.

Here again, the explosion must come from everyone.

We must know in advance that we do not know the manifestations and the modalities of it.

Faced with a boss who performs a "personal" and "revolutionary" righteous act for Christ by lodging a family of his workers in his house, contrary to all customs, the militant Christian worker might risk telling him: "It will weaken the spirit of struggle in the workers, thus the effectiveness of the liberation of the working class."

This would be grave. This would be the opposite of the "world program"—it would be to condemn a small manifestation of the Spirit of God. It would be to condemn a little of the Kingdom of Heaven established in man's heart in the name of some possible human betterment.

It is however, in all likelihood, by approaches of this kind, groping and fragmented, that in "doing the good" some Christians who are *"in the world"* just like the little and the oppressed "move toward the light" and will cease to be *"of the world"*.

The Mission must not forget that it is "for all creatures".

If those who suffer, because of the very structure of the world, from sometimes unheard-of human hardships have the right to the proclamation of salvation, then those who, under the weight of the same structure, suffer monstrous supernatural hardships—those who *commit* injustice as if by force, oppressing, disdaining, solely on account of the social machinery in which their destiny has placed them—those have almost more right, because they are more than poor: they are sinners.

To refuse them the love of compassion and salvation is to separate oneself from the heart of Christ.

Blessed Are the Meek [13]

Our realm is overrun by injustice.

The responses of the world to injustice are all either active violence or consent.

To establish the meekness of Christ here is a scandal.

Who can measure the courage required of those who would consent to carry out this scandal of meekness?

But is there any greater or truer scandal than this one, that Christians left to someone like Gandhi the responsibility of raising up a mass of men in the world who trust themselves to the uncontrollable force of this Meekness?

And yet, here again it is not a choice. The "meek and humble of heart" Christ is a fact. We can neither adjust nor adapt him.

3. The Thought of Christ

We are not free thinkers.

In the sector of the world where we are, we are not free to allow the thought of Christ to be modified by the thought of the world: and this is not always easy.

Perhaps it is useful to recall certain aspects of this thought:

The love of Christ is universal.

All love of those who take the love of others away from us is not the love of Christ.

[13] Mt 5:4.

Poverty is not linked to a low salary (cf. the personal relations of Christ with some rich people). It is the state of the one who does not hoard and who does not hoard because of the need of others.

Evangelical poverty is not that of a particular class, of a particular profession. It is beyond all of that.

It is much more about not planning for the future than about insecurity.

"Do not be anxious . . ."[14]

That is why the effort for the Kingdom and for an economic system cannot be entirely aligned.

"Evangelic" work is not human work.

"My Father is working still . . ."[15]

The "mystery of work" does not have value in and of itself.

In the Gospel, Christ does not speak of human work except on occasion in the parables on the Work of the Kingdom of Heaven.

Christ's public life is absolutely brimming with prodigious activity, but this activity is connected neither to money nor to any kind of human work.

However, in that life, as in that of the Apostles, "you will earn your bread by the sweat of your brow"[16] is supremely respected.

The notion of work, which is always welded to that of efficiency, is lived on a transcendent level for an efficacy that surpasses human ability.

[14] Mt 6:25.
[15] Jn 5:17.
[16] Gen 3:19.

Evangelic work is a constant movement toward the meeting of men in order to "scatter among them" the seed of the Kingdom of God.

All great human activities have the value of signs.

Just as marriage is the most perfect sign of the union between Christ and his Church, and voluntary celibacy makes us live more fully the reality indicated by this sign, human work is the sign of the great labor of the Church for the world, suffering and efficacious labor.

This labor is ours.

It places us at equal distance from a work that would be absolute and an idleness that would be sterile.

Here, as elsewhere, the sign must remain in its place and not hide the reality.

The Unfortunate

We must not shrink mercy to fit the fashion of the day.[17]

For Christ, the sorrowful are:

sinners

the bereaved

the sick

the little ones

and among these little ones, the poor, but not only in money.

We do not have the right to make a correction and call only certain ones poor.

---

[17] The three sentences that follow from "For Christ" to "heart of Christ" are absent from the 1966 edition and the 1995 paperback edition.

If there are poor in money, there are poor in love, gifts, strengths. We owe them the heart of Christ.[18]

Awareness of the economic misfortune of the masses must not lead us to disdain other forms of misfortune, to be uninterested in them.

The mercy of Christ for the poor is part of a mercy as vast as all human woe.

It is mercy to sinners,
mercy to the sick,
mercy to those who mourn their dead,
mercy to captives,
mercy to everyone who is a little.

Because of a materialized notion of poverty, we often risk forgetting that there are other kinds of poverty besides the economically poor, other little ones besides proletariats.

There are the morally or psychologically infirm.

There are those poor in gifts, attractiveness, love.

Alongside oppressed classes, there are the "unclass-able".

The poor and the little are not only in the proletariat.

And the proletariat itself is not exclusively composed of militants, those militants already rich with a hope, a richness of heart, a formation of spirit.

Neither can the heart of Christ be modified; it is for everyone and it is to everyone that we have to give it.

---

[18] Madeleine Delbrêl wrote in the margin: "Love: I know . . ."

This personal love of Christ "calls his own sheep by name".[19] It does not call a category.

He knows each one "as the Father knows the Son".[20]

We have to rediscover this personal love between someone and someone else.

This love is mutilated by the labels that we plaster onto our brothers, according to whether they were born here or there, whether they live here or there, and by the "social" definition that we give ourselves. We no longer know how to meet as a man meets a man in his singular simplicity.

We no longer know how to call by name.

Finally, the last possible infiltration: the truth of Christ is *free of success*.

The number of those who come to it does not change it.

On the other hand, it is not a matter of generosity: the love of some people for a particular doctrine that would make us transfer to this doctrine the admiration we have for them.

Let us say it again: this perception of the Christian life—and because it is Christian, the missionary life— does not pretend to be, and should not be, the same for everyone.

We do not deny that the Holy Spirit wants others situated in another perspective. Everyone lives what each person lives.

[19] Jn 10:3.
[20] Cf. Mt 11:27, Jn 10:15.

But while the Church, simultaneously and perpetually, has to live the Figures who lived and wrote as a sign of her, we would voluntarily say that our place in her is on the path of the Exodus.

As others have to live the exile and servitude of all the Egypts, as still others have to gravitate toward the frontiers of the Promised Land, it seems we have to live the journeys of the Desert.

In order to leave Egypt, you have to be there.

In order to leave Egypt, you have to pull yourself away from it.

In all the ages of her history, the Church has carried people, perpetual nomads, within her who constantly leave the world where they are but of which they are not, toward this earth where, through Christ, they already are.

Of them we might say that we do not know "either where they are from or where they are going"[21] in a world where they remain equally brothers and strangers.

They know that they walk in the one who is "the road", the road that is without signposts and without inns but that is full of manna and living springs because:

The Exodus is not only an event of the past. The Church always travels by the same paths. Until all the families of the earth are gathered together and blessed in the Bosom of Abraham, that is to say, in

[21] Parallel to the wind from Jn 3:8.

Christ, the People of God must constantly leave behind the idolatrous servitude of Egypt, constantly walk in the austerity of the Desert, constantly try to gain the Promised Land. Until the Second Coming, the Church is always in the Desert. She never ceases to regret [the loss of] Egyptian conveniences, even with murmuring in her midst or sin among her leaders, but God who is faithful infallibly pushes her forward by punishment and pardon up to the new heaven and new earth that Jesus will usher in on the day of his Second Coming.[22]

[22] We do not know the author of this quote.